Political Leadership in Africa

Volume One

PATRICE LUMUMBA
AHEAD OF HIS TIME

DIDIER NDONGALA MUMBATA

ISBN 978-1-78222-933-9

Book design, layout and production management by Into Print
www.intoprint.net, +44 (0)1604 832140

Second printing 2022

CONTENTS

PREFACE

IN 1997, WHILE TAKING COURSES in Political Language, Rhetoric and Propaganda, political economy and Political Leadership at the Institute of Political Science at University of Copenhagen, I realized that the American and European students, who were taking the same courses as I was, knew very little about Africa, its history, its people and its geography. Indeed, in Political Leadership courses, the study focuses on extraordinary political leaders who have shaped world history, such as Niccolo Machiavelli, Napoleon Bonaparte, John Fitzgerald Kennedy, Martin Luther King, Adolf Hitler, Vladimir Ilich Ulyanov Lenin, Thomas Woodrow Wilson, Mahatma Ghandi, Julius Caesar, Thomas Jefferson, Abraham Lincoln, Joan of Arc, Genghis Khan, etc. The list is very long, but no African leader is mentioned.

Thus, for many Americans and Europeans, Africa began to exist through the colonization, and it is usually the crises that absorb the attention of headlines, writers and television commentators in Europe, in America, and the rest of the world. In comparison, little attention is paid to Africa's success stories, and yet they abound. In fact, African societies had achieved various levels of political sophistication long before colonization. They were organized, from the simplest to the most complex forms, into bands, lineages, chieftaincies, kingdoms and empires.

The main purpose of this book is to make known the great African political leaders in the world and that all the peoples of the world take a new look at the role of political leadership in African political life. The old myths that Africans had no history of their own, that they had not developed any political, social or economic systems before the arrival of Europeans, are no longer credible. Evidence of Africa's own history exists in many forms, in archaeology, in language structures, in artefacts of life and work, in building styles, in social and economic customs and structures, in oral traditions, in art and writing. The history or the question of colonization of Africa is so complex. But everyone seems to completely forget that it is the inhabitants of this continent who invented, billions of years ago, mathematics, medicine, architecture, writing, civilization, etc. And any sensible person cannot understand how the Europeans claimed to have civilized Africa, a continent which, long before their arrival and long before them, had invented civilization. What a paradox!

And as far as records of historical events are concerned, many African political leaders can be considered candidates for the role of historical political heroes, great men such as Soundiata Keita, the Mani Kongo Nzinga Nkuvu, Gamal Abdel Nasser, Kwame Nkrumah, Leopold Sedar Senghor, Patrice Emery Lumumba, Nelson Rolihlahla Mandela, Nimi A Lukeni, Almamy Samory Toure, Chaka Zulu, Kimpa Vita Nsimba, Simon Kimbangu, Mansa Kanga Mousa and so on. Each of them, in one way or another, has influenced historical events and shaped the history of Africa. For example, Mansa Kanga Moussa, the king of Mali from 1312 to 1337, an empire in West Africa, is considered the richest man in the history of mankind with more than 400 billion dollars, because until today, no one has possessed such a sum of money.

This first volume of books on Political Leadership in Africa is dedicated to the Congolese political leader Patrice Emery Lumumba, how he appeared in Congolese political life, how he shaped world history, what people thought of him, and what he accomplished. Politicians, journalists, and even academics tend to formulate observations about political behaviour in terms of the thoughts and actions of leading personalities associated with particular societies and particular historic eras. I sincerely believe that the tendency to focus on dominant personalities to explain political behaviour is even more prevalent in the case of recent African history than it has been in many other parts of the world. For, in the face of weak institutions and kaleidoscopic political scenes, the extended tenure of some African political leaders provides a somewhat stable hook for political analysis. Indeed, the influence of Patrice Lumumba on the life of Congolese, on the way the Congolese have thought and acted, deserves to be analysed politically. The consequences of the events that led to the independence of Congo would have been profoundly different if he had not acted as he did. He was certainly an exceptional political leader, but unfortunately he arrived too early on the political scene of the Democratic Republic of Congo.

This country has undergone several name changes, from the Independent State of Congo in 1885, to Belgian Congo in 1908, to the Republic of Congo in 1960, to the Democratic Republic of Congo in 1961, to the Republic of Zaire in 1971, and again to the Democratic Republic of Congo in 1997. It is the second largest country in Africa after Algeria, and more than 300 ethnic groups, speaking between 300 and 600 dialects and languages, live there. Prior to European colonization, the peoples of Congo were part of empires, kingdoms, and small communities of forest villages. Perhaps the most famous kingdom was the Kongo, established as early as the 13th century. This Christian kingdom had diplomatic relations with Portugal, Spain and the Vatican. To the east, the emperor of the Lunda Empire maintained relations with the Portuguese and traded with Arabs.

The completion of this book would not have been possible without a great help. I am indebted to some writers, for their books have broadened my knowledge and enhanced my understanding of Africa, a continent immensely rich in natural resources. Many Congolese, as witnesses of the 1950s and 1960s events, should be given special recognition for the ideas which came to fruition in this study. Among those to whom I owe much because of their guidance and inspiration are my father Paul Ndongala Nzinga Mumbata, one of the Congolese "évolués" (educated and westernized Congolese) and my mother Germaine Madiensi Mandina, one of the few Congolese women teachers in the 1950s. Finally, I am grateful to Professor Dr. Tom Bryder, director of International Study Programs in Denmark, for his valuable help and encouragement.

INTRODUCTION

ALTHOUGH EACH COUNTRY HAS ITS own particular authority structure, leaders and leadership have always constituted an inescapable part of human social existence at all levels of society. Indeed, leadership becomes necessary for the success and survival of any organization. It is conceived as a form of influence or persuasion and as a function of a group process or a function of individual personality. In general, political leadership is different from other forms of leadership. It means the control of policies that affect the welfare of the population and also the ability to transform a strong public sentiment into a personal crusade.

A potential political leader controls attributes that are rare but admired and that allow him or her to claim pre-eminence over others in society. His or her pre-eminence establishes a set of rights, privileges, duties, and patterns of behaviour that properly set him or her apart from the masses. But does an exceptional political leader really shape human history? Or does history inevitably sweep us all along in its wake? The reality is certainly more complex. Perhaps there has to be a fit between the individual and the social environment for leadership and social evolution to occur. A given genius can come either too early or too late.

However, in some cases, individuals certainly do have a profound impact on political outcomes. It is clear that the impact that some great men had on the political outcomes of their time was vastly disproportionate to the impact exerted by other individuals operating during the same periods. These were "event-making" leaders whose actions were the consequences of exceptional abilities of intelligence, will and character rather than of accidents of position. They succeeded in making their mark on history through their ability to organize and sustain activities that led to the implementation of their ideas and programs. For better or for worse, they have been able effectively to draw attention to the critical needs and problems of the time, to communicate with the members of the politically relevant strata of that society, and to mobilize both the human and material resources necessary to achieve important goals; as a result, they have been able to create extraordinary and new things.

Therefore, everywhere in the inhabited world, in all times and circumstances, the myths of a man have flourished. In Congo-Kinshasa, the most striking feature of the political scene has been the personality of Patrice Lumumba. In the 1950s and until his assassination on January 17, 1961, he was undoubtedly the greatest leader of Congo in modern times. His charismatic hold on the Congolese masses was a reality in Africa and the rest of the world. He represented a whole generation of young Congolese who reached a certain maturity and who provided political leadership to the struggle for independence. Very early in his political life, Patrice Lumumba manifested the characteristics of a man born to lead. He lived as a free man and an independent thinker. Everything he wrote, said or did was the product of someone who knew that his vocation was that of a liberator. An insatiable reader, he pursued his education by teaching himself a wide range of subjects, including law, economics and philosophy. He was truly an exceptional man or genius. Such men always have exceptional qualities that can place them above others. But, they also have Failings that can eventually destroy them.

Lumumba's forthright pan-Africanism and unconditional dedication to Congo made him an enemy of the Western powers, especially the United States of America and Belgium, the colonial power. He had only one idea in mind: to fight for independence is to fight for national unity. He believed that political independence should naturally be based on economic and social freedom. He therefore resisted all forms of external control, calling instead for the Congolese to rely on their own strength. An ardent Congolese nationalist, he sought to preserve the integrity of a nation threatened by ethnic conflict, regional fragmentation, labour unrest, bureaucratic collapse, military mutinies, and international interference. Although these difficulties proved insurmountable, allowing his enemies to arrest and assassinate him, he is today revered as a heroic martyr of African independence and a powerful symbol against imperialism.

CHAPTER I

EMERGENCE OF A CONGOLESE ELITE

THE PROCESS OF THE EMERGENCE of the Congolese elite can be linked to major events, such as the struggle for independence, the workers' strike and resistance movements, which led to the creation of all kinds of organizations. And to understand the social milieu that produced Patrice Lumumba's leadership, it is necessary to highlight a number of historical realities that left a deep imprint on the Congolese political elite.

The imposition of European administration, commerce and religion on traditional Congolese life led to the rise of protest and resistance movements.

There have been cases of armed resistance among the Azande in the northeast of Congo, the Yaka in the southwest, the Luba-Katanga in the southeast, etc. In addition, there have been isolated uprisings in response to specific local abuses of the Congolese population. Contrary to widespread myth, Patrice Lumumba's Tetela tribe, as a group, did not rise up against the establishment and consolidation of colonial rule, and much of the rebel activity took place outside Tetela territory, although many of the rebels on both sides of the Lualaba were Tetela. In any case, resistance among all these peoples was more or less continuous, beginning under the Congo Independent State and continuing through the early years after annexation. But unfortunately, the Congolese had no formal political means of collective expression in the early colonial period, mainly because by the time the Europeans decided to annex Congo, the power of most centralized pre-colonial states had reached its peak. The powerful kingdoms and empires, such as Kongo, Lunda, Kuba, Luba, etc, were unfortunately too weak to organize a sustained armed resistance against well-organized European-led armies.

However, political protest was often organized by religious movements and separatist churches that affirmed Congolese values. The most famous of these was Kimbanguism, which is generally considered the most important independent Christian religious movement in Central Africa. Simon Kimbangu was inspired by the Anthonian sect, a messianic black consciousness movement led by a young female prophet named Kimpa Vita Nsimba, born in 1684 and known in European history books as Dona Beatriz. In the 1700s, Kimpa Vita defined her mission as restoring the Kongo kingdom to its former glory and purity. She was convicted of heresy and burned at the stake on July 2, 1706. But her vision of African renaissance and black power would be shared by modern Congolese prophets, beginning with Simon Kimbangu.

Although he was active for only a few months before being arrested by the colonial government, Simon Kimbangu, born on September 12, 1887 in Nkamba, developed a religious movement that later grew into a large, well-organized church called "the Church of Jesus Christ on Earth by Prophet Simon Kimbangu", but well known in Africa and elsewhere as Kimbanguism. And this new church became a member of the World council of churches in 1969. It all began in 1921 when Simon Kimbangu had a dream that he was appointed by God to heal illness and preach the gospel of liberation from all forms of oppression, including sorcery, other negative customs and white domination. This sect, which arose spontaneously and almost overnight, became a resistance group directed against European government and interests, as well as against the Catholic and Protestant missionary churches. Kimbangu was arrested in September 1921, accused of having committed, according to the Belgian colonizers, a crime against state security for having preached the subversive ideas of pan-Africanism. When tried, he was sentenced to life imprisonment and, isolated, he died on October 12, 1951 in prison in Lubumbashi (Elisabethville). But his prophetic ministry continued to influence the course of events in Congo. The model set by Kimbangu was followed by a number of preachers, teachers, workers and school children who later became politicians. These forms of popular resistance against colonial tyranny would influence not only the struggle for independence, but also the current quest for true democracy in Congo.

The post-war period brought new challenges to endure on the Belgian colonialism. The administration of the colony was restructured. Several decrees were issued reorganizing the chiefdoms, sectors and "indigenous districts". The large states and ethnic groups were divided into manageable units, while the smaller decentralized peoples were grouped into chiefdoms created by the Belgian colonizers. As a result, the Congolese people gradually lost the right to take initiatives on their own, crushed by the weight of the three facets of colonial power that included the colonial bureaucracy, the concessionary companies and the religious missions. Travel outside the native region, for example, was strictly regulated and every individual wishing to travel had to obtain a travel permit. The Congolese sometimes rebelled against the rigors of colonial oppression. In 1931, the Pende of Kwilu rebelled against high taxes, low wages in the palm oil industry and the interference of the colonial administration in traditional political affairs. In 1941, a miners' strike in Lubumbashi ended with the shooting of strikers. Similarly, a revolt by "Force Publique" soldiers in Kananga in 1944 resulted in violent repression. In effect, Belgium, being supported by all tree facets of colonial power, practiced a form of pragmatic paternalism, claiming that it only dominated the Congolese in order to serve them better; the colonial state regulated the social behaviour of the Congolese; the concessionary companies employed the Congolese in menial, low-paying jobs; and the religious missions educated and socialized the Congolese to accept their subordination.

Meanwhile, in the post-war period, Belgium began to cultivate a selective Congolese bourgeoisie with the intention of creating an indigenous "buffer" class, educated in Belgian culture and supporting the colonial system. A truly separate social class situated between the two communities, the Belgians and the backward Congolese mass, since because of the policy of racial segregation instituted by Belgium in Congo, Whites and Blacks did not socialize. Thus, there were some fairly fortunate Congolese who had access to education beyond the elementary level, primarily in Catholic or Protestant mission schools. The Belgians called them "évolués" (educated and westernized Congolese) in order to distinguish them from the rest of the population. In fact, Congo was the country of two groups of "évolués". The holders of the "immatriculation" card constituted a new class of Congolese who were allowed to enter European restaurants, nightclubs and cinemas, and also to send their children to European schools. Holders of "merite civique" card, available upon request, were Congolese who felt sufficiently detribalized and wanted additional privileges. In 1956, only 120 Congolese out of a population of sixteen million held a "immatriculation" card and less than 900 held a "merite civique" card.

In reality, the emergence of the "évolués" had been favoured by the circumstances of the Second World War, which made it impossible to recruit new agents in Europe because of the separation between Congo and Belgium. To fill the gap, more and more Congolese had to be used and given responsibilities that had previously been reserved for whites only. This is how the European junior staff was replaced by black auxiliary personnel. However, a new political consciousness took hold of the Congolese "évolués". Subsequently, they formed cultural associations, either of a tribal character or composed of interest groups. These associations, included UNELMA (Union of Former

Students of the Marist Brothers), ASSANEF (Association of Former Students of the brothers of the Christian schools), ABAKO (The Bakongo Alliance), UNISCO (Union of Congolese social interest), ADAPES (former students of the scheut fathers), etc, constituted privileged movements that had the effect of sharpening the political consciousness of the nation. The Congolese "évolués" began to question their true role in the Belgian system and demanded equal treatment with the Europeans. They insisted on better educational opportunities for the Congolese.

Despite the fact that few Catholics saw the need for higher education outside the seminaries, the majority of missionaries did not support the demands of this new elite. By the mid-1950s, the "évolués" had developed a real political consciousness, noticing that the issues most important to them had often been ignored. As a result, they were disappointed very quickly. They understood perfectly well that the institution of the "immatriculation" or "mérite civique" card did not honour the Congolese. No country in the world issued cards to distinguish the elites from the masses. Belgium's primary intention was to divide the Congolese population in order to rule better. For those who obtained these cards were not totally assimilated to whites. As far as the professional contract was concerned, the black man was covered by the contract of employment, whatever his activities were. The white man, whether he was an intellectual or a manual worker, or the least paid, benefited from the employment contract, which always allowed him to receive higher remuneration and allowances than those of the most highly paid black man.

Also, despite their cards, the "évolués" were hardly accepted in European restaurants, cinemas, hotels and bars. They clearly understood long ago that they did not live in the best of worlds. For the Congolese who had the chance to travel to Central and West Africa, as well as to Europe, noted with bitterness that there was no racial segregation there. This was the shock that Patrice Lumumba felt in 1947 when he returned from Brazzaville and in 1958 when he returned from Accra. This is probably what changed his political vision. Totally disillusioned by the Belgian colonialists, the "évolués" wanted to remain Congolese with their good customs and languages, not carbon copies of white people. Internally, pressure from the colonial regime created a spirit of unrest that was increasingly felt among the population. Then in 1954, Auguste Buisseret, a liberal politician, was appointed Minister of the Colonies. As soon as he was installed, he introduced new administrative policies and disassociated himself from the Catholic Church, which ran many educational and social programs in Congo. The opposition of the Catholic missionaries to his policy revealed for the first time to the Congolese people the existence of dissensions between Catholics and Liberals, and between Flemish and Walloons.

At that time, settled in Kisangani, Patrice Lumumba entered the ranks of the Congolese évolués class. He sought and obtained the "immatriculation" card. At that time, his political opinions were those of a moderate, as shown in the book "Congo, my country" that he wrote in the years 1956-57, he admired the achievements of the Belgians that he tried to imitate. The man who would later become the greatest hero and martyr of Congo's independence was at the time one of the supporters of a Belgian-Congolese community. Nevertheless, he was deeply aware that Belgians rarely considered the Congolese as their equals. Many of the "évolués", however, were very keen to improve their own status and income, and to differentiate themselves socially and politically from the masse of backward natives. Until 1956, their main interests revolved around "human relations" or their quest for full integration into colonial or white society. They adhered to the vision of a Belgian-Congolese community in which they would become partners with the colonialists in order to rule over the "ignorant mass".

As a result, upon Congo's independence, when most of the "évolués" quickly rose to positions of leadership, their main objective was to dominate the masses. The majority of these newly elected political leaders were more concerned with enjoying the material privileges that colonialism had denied them. As representatives of the people, their first official act was to accept not only the privileges enjoyed by the Belgians before them, but also some new privileges of their own creation. Parliamentarians, for example, voted to increase their salaries. The new Congolese politicians, who had replaced the Belgians as rulers and administrators, were just as bad, oppressive and cruel. They lived in large colonial mansions or villas, drove nice cars, sometimes bigger and nicer cars than those of the colonialists, despised the people, and did not hesitate to use the army and police to suppress any dissent or challenge to their authority. In many cases, their use of force was unjustified and totally arbitrary. They were the "new whites", black in skin but white in thought.

With such politicians in charge of the country, I can clearly understand now why the Democratic Republic of Congo collapsed politically, economically and socially only shortly after independence and became a new theatre of war, competition between political leaders, conflict and hostility between tribes. The dramatic consequence of their behaviour was a very long period of political and economic instability in the country. Unfortunately for Congo, only a few politicians behaved differently and among them, Patrice Emery

Lumumba. Although full of good intentions, the Congolese Prime Minister did not have the resources necessary to prevent what was happening in Congo. What could he do alone against the powerful Americans, Belgians and their allies who were truly determined to remove him from power at all costs and install a puppet government instead? Anyway, Patrice Lumumba was so concerned with improving the living standards of his people that his own life was meaningless if he could not succeed. In other words, he was willing to suffer and die for his people.

Main influences on Congolese leaders, and education

The influence of the family is difficult to assess in the case of the Congolese elite, but very realistic. And despite aggressive colonization, the subsequent creation of a national identity and the conversion of many Congolese to Christianity, many aspects of various Congolese beliefs and practices have survived. For example, the Kongo, Bete, Teke, Kuba, and Songye used figurines with all sorts of accessories, medicinal plants, and also the mastery of power to meet the needs of individuals or groups. These figurines varied in size, gesture, and accessories depending on the powers they were supposed to master, harness, and the activities they were supposed to help people undertake. Some healed diseases, others blocked misfortunes.

In most traditional Congolese societies, members were distinguished according to a scale of value or merit. Age was generally respected, as was wealth, political or religious office, and prowess in such areas as hunting, warfare and storytelling. Almost everyone participated in initiations, the ceremonies that marked a change in status, position, or role for an individual or group. Upon taking office, a Kongo chief had to undergo an elaborate initiation. This included a period of seclusion and a test to ascertain the approval of the spiritual forces and their willingness to confer some of their powers on the new chief. Unlike the Kongo, Patrice Lumumba's tribe, the Tetela, had no centralized political authority. Leadership was provided by a council of elders from a complex, multi-level institution dedicated to the development of moral behaviour, to which most Tetela men and women belonged. Advancement within the society was based on a series of payments and demonstrations of knowledge about Tetela culture appropriate to each rank. During these traditional Congolese ceremonies, an initiate would learn the necessary information from a variety of sources, including proverbs, songs, and the manipulation of various objects, both natural and human-made. The oral tradition was very rich in poems and songs that celebrated community life and gave advice on how to live in harmony with community members. Folk tales, which usually focused on an element of wisdom, were an essential part of a child's education, as were proverbs. These proverbs dealt with all aspects of life, including the importance of family, respect for authority and the mutual obligations of community members.

However, it is clear that most members of the Congolese elite came from large extended families, mostly of peasant origin, but some in the process of urbanization. They were brought or came to the city themselves as very young children. Life in the city and the urbanization process itself was a traumatic experience for the child and the family as well. Living in the city, they had the opportunity to meet strangers or visitors who gave them cause to think and aggravated their frustration of having to endure the bitterness of the colonial situation that they unfortunately could not change. One of them, Felix Eboue, an African, born in Guyana on January 1, 1884 and living in Brazzaville in the 1940s, was Governor General of French Equatorial Africa from 1941 to 1944, and an early Resistance fighter during the Second World War. He died on May 17, 1944 in Egypt and has been buried in the Panthéon since May 20, 1949. When Eboue and his family made an official visit to Kinshasa in the early 1940s, all Congolese were proud to see a black man treated with such respect by the same Belgians who had no regard for them. From that moment on, they were convinced that one day the Belgians would respect them in the same way they respected Eboue, if only they could fight for it.

The rapid growth of nationalist sentiment among the Congolese was also due in part to the writings of a young Belgian professor at the University of Antwerp's Overseas Territories Institute, A.J. van Bilsen, who published a proposal for the independence of Congo. In December 1955, he published the so-called "thirty year plan". In this plan, he proposed that the peoples of Congo should be gradually prepared for autonomy over the next three decades. Although Belgian officials dismissed van Bilsen's proposal as an idealistic dream, the Congolese were deeply moved by a statement about their independence in a specific number of years. In response to van Bilsen, the Kinshasa periodical "Conscience Africaine", which reflected the thinking of the Bangala elite, published a "manifesto" in its July-August 1956 issue. Generally sympathetic to van Bilsen's ideas, the "manifesto" called on the Congolese to participate in making plans for the future of Congo. But on August 23, 1956, a "counter-manifesto" was printed by the ABAKO (Association of Bakongo).

Rejecting the concept of a slow evolution of the Congolese people within the framework of a plan conceived in Belgium, the ABAKO pleaded for an immediate independence of the Congolese.

The influence of the Brussels International Exhibition on the Congolese is difficult to estimate. When it was organized in April 1958, Belgium lifted its colonial barriers to let a few hundred of Congolese through. The number of these Congolese who visited Europe on the occasion of the World's Fair was about one hundred times greater than the total number of those who have come to Belgium since then. Coming from different regions of the colony, regions between which movement was strictly regulated, they were able to meet for the first time in the capital of Belgium and had the opportunity to make contact with men and women of all nations and races. They discovered that no people or race has a monopoly on virtue or vice. For the first time, they spoke on equal terms with Europeans, Americans and Asians. Having been to Belgium, they discovered that it was a country like any other, with good and bad sides.

Some Congolese took advantage of this opportunity to become familiar with the Belgian "Left" that advocated the independence for Congo. Therefore, they were already determined not to accept the colonial joke anymore. Meanwhile, nationalist sentiment began to grow among them. Young Congolese, like Patrice Lumumba, began to realize how much they had been kept apart from the rest of the world. Lumumba came into contact with Africans from countries such as Ghana and Guinea that had already gained independence, and with Africans from the French colonies who had elected representatives to the French government and were about to receive some form of autonomy. This contact with more mature independence movements would have been an important factor in preparing the ground for Lumumba's and others Congolese leaders' demands for immediate independence from late 1958.

In addition, the Congolese were certainly inspired by the nationalist struggles that were being waged in other parts of the continent, in Ghana, Guinea, Egypt and elsewhere, and in particular, to the transformation of the French Congo, just across the river, into the Republic of Congo with a promise of independence from French president Charles De Gaulle when he returned to power in May 1958. Independence became a real possibility for most of the French colonies in West and Central Africa when a referendum was held in those territories on September 28, 1958. The African colonies were asked to vote on whether they wanted to remain part of the French community. As a result, the Governor General of the Belgian Congo, Henri Cornelis, received a petition signed by several Congolese intellectuals asking the Belgian authorities to show the same understanding attitude as the French president de Gaulle. But the French colonies, with the exception of Algeria, were not characterized by a significant European settlement. On the contrary, in the Belgian Congo, the participation of white settlers was significant. Therefore, Belgium only reluctantly began to entertain the idea of a black majority rule and the independence in the late 1950s. Before 1957, the Congolese were involved in politics only through their association with Belgian political groups that had established branches in the colony and through ethnic associations.

Although the colonial system was often justified by its "civilizing mission", the Belgian government was adamantly opposed to providing the kind of education deemed necessary to transform the "native" into a "civilized" person. The religious missions, both Catholic and Protestant, were responsible for providing education to all Congolese children. But the primary purpose of education was to train the Congolese for tasks that would be useful to European businesses. Secondary education was limited only to those Congolese who were to serve as clergymen, teachers, or non-commissioned officers in the army. There were no Congolese doctors, dentists, pharmacists or lawyers in the Belgian Congo. No Congolese attended university or studied in Europe until the 1950s, a factor that may explain in part the absence of a nascent nationalist movement in the years immediately following World War II.

Secondary and University education was not made available to the Congolese early enough to enable them to develop a broad cadre of administrators capable of taking charge of the country at independence. Only a small number of Congolese succeeded as business owners, planters, breeders, and small-scale manufacturers. For example, in the village of Ngeba, in the Bas-Congo region where my mother is from, a mechanized woodworking shop (the Ngeba manufacturer) employed about twenty people. Further east in Congo, Joseph Kapend Tshombe, Moise Tshombe's father, built his family's fortune and the foundations of a small business empire by organizing the import of cassava from Kasai province into Katanga province. He became the first Congolese millionaire in Belgian francs and travelled to Belgium in 1948, at a time when travel restrictions were severe for Congolese.

It is significant that a large part of the future Congolese Elite attended religious schools, especially catholic ones. Christian missionary activity had a profound impact on traditional life in Congo, both Protestants and Catholics were willing to eradicate indigenous customs. As a result, these schools were often centers of unrest. By 1948, educational reforms had been made in Congo. A full six years secondary program was instituted for the first time.

Subsequently, three groups of Congolese, Catholic priests, medical assistants, and agricultural assistants, entered professions requiring post-secondary education, with the degrees of the first two categories being roughly equivalent to a university degree. But the rest of the Congolese elite did not have such impressive formal education credentials. The maximum level of education in this group was a secondary school diploma, for which three to six years of post-primary education were required, depending on the professional qualifications needed. However, the intellectual credentials of Congolese political leaders were not exclusively a function of formal education achievements. Many of them read extensively on their own or took correspondence courses. Patrice Emery Lumumba was an autodidact whose formal education consisted of only six years of elementary school, four years of secondary school and one year of technical training at a postal clerk school.

The establishment of a complete university education in Congo began with the creation of the Louvanium University in 1954 in Kinshasa and the University of Lubumbashi in 1956. In December 1958, there were 248 Congolese students at Louvanium and 42 at Lubumbashi. But since1952, Congolese students were already taking courses at the University of Louvain and the Université libre in Belgium. On July 9, 1954, Emile Adolphe Disengomoka received his dipoma of Literary Regent at the Regency School of Nivelles in Belgium, a diploma that no Congolese had obtained until then, and two years later, in 1956, Thomas Kanza received a diploma in psychology at the University of Louvain. Few Congolese were able to attend secondary school or university. As a result, at independence there were fewer than 30,000 students enrolled in secondary education (two per cent of the total), fewer than 200 secondary school graduates and only about 20 Congolese with university degree. Although, Congolese students, particularly university students, had little influence in the early years after independence, they organized themselves into associations and formed significant blocs in some political parties in the mid-1960s. Many of them supported Patrice Lumumba and were deeply saddened and angered by his assassination in 1961.

Patrice Emery Lumumba was born on July 2, 1925 into a family of Tetela peasants in the village of Onalua, 300 km northeast of the province of Katanga, in the territory of Katako-Kombe, Sankuru district, province of Kasai. His parents were Catholic, married in the church, and had four children, all boys, raised in catholic doctrine. Meanwhile, Lumumba was educated in a Protestant elementary school in his village. There, the young Lumumba rebelled against the paternalism and authoritarianism of the Catholic and

Protestant missionaries in Sankuru and fled to Kindu in the province of Haut-Congo. One day, while being interviewed by journalists, Lumumba declared that he had always been against injustice since his youth. He received a thorough education in Christian doctrine and was always a sensitive person. His parents told him to always be kind to people and never hit back when someone hits you. Therefore, he could never understand why, in his country, at school, they were taught to be good, to be charitable, to love their neighbour by the same Belgians who treated them very badly. How to reconcile what the Belgians taught them at school, the principles of civilisation and morality, with what they were doing to the Congolese population? And by making this observation on a daily basis, by comparing what they were teaching them with what they were doing, Lumumba came up against a contradiction every time. Therefore, he became aware and began to study revolutions throughout humanity in general. He often looked at the French Revolution and what was behind it. Why did the people of France revolt? They wanted their freedom. He found a common thread in all these revolutions: the struggle against injustice and repression.

For a short time, Lumumba lived in Kindu and was active in the local group of "évolués". According to his close friends, Kindu had an essential influence on Lumumba's desire to become a politician. After attending a Roman Catholic normal school in Kinshasa (Leopoldville), he moved to Kisangani (Stanleyville) where he began working at the age of 19 as a tax clerk, before moving to the postal service. In 1956, he was president of the "évolués" club of Kisangani, provincial president of APIC (association of native personnel of the colony), a union founded in 1946 to express demands for African promotion and fair wages. He was president of a section of ADAPES (Association of Former Students of the Scheut Fathers) and president of a Tetela ethnic group (Tetela Mutual). In addition, Patrice Lumumba was also president of the Belgian-Congolese cultural group. He demonstrated great energy and organizational skills as president of these cultural, educational and professional groups. Through the activities of these associations, he learned a lot about the world, as well as about the art of organizing, and he also acquired in the process a strong commitment to the political emancipation and economic development of the Congo as a multi-ethnic state. During this period, Lumumba read avidly and was the dominant personality among the Congolese in Kisangani. He was a frequent contributor to various magazines and newspapers, including "la croix du Congo", and "la voix du Congolais". His powers of observation and eloquence impressed all his friends and aroused fear and criticism. He had an uncanny ability to deal with difficult situations and was often able to impress people who were thought to be better informed and educated than he was. His thirst for knowledge was insatiable; he was a voracious reader and, to a large extent, self-taught. He was aided in this by European friends who provided him with books and periodicals from abroad.

In Kisangani, Lumumba, tall, slim, always well dressed and sociable, was very present on the political scene. The colonial authorities considered him somewhat dangerous and watched him closely. In 1956, Lumumba was one of the Congolese invited to Brussels for consultations on the drafting of the Uniform code to governing public employment. Upon his return to Congo, he was arrested, convicted of theft at the post office and sentenced to two years in prison by a district court. Many colonial Belgians were eager to prevent his rise in popularity and power. He appealed and was transferred to Kinshasa. Meanwhile, in Belgium, the supporters of colonial reform, some journalists and politicians found the affair an ideal opportunity to discredit the colonial administration. In 1957, the court reduced Lumumba's two years prison sentence to six months, which he had already served. Once released from prison, he became more popular. He resumed his activities as an influential leader of the independence movement. He stayed in Kinshasa where his Belgian friends found him a job as commercial director of the Bracongo brewery well known for the name of its beer "Polar". Lumumba was enormously successful in this job, as he was a born leader and had an amazing organizational ability. He succeeded in making Polar the favorite drink in the city instead of Primus, its rival.

Although Lumumba was extremely successful as a business manager, the rapid changes in Congo allowed him to use his organizational and promotional skills in politics, a new field that had just opened up to the Congolese. The Belgian government restructured urban areas to allow limited Congolese participation in municipal affairs and organized elections in December 1957 in the Congolese communes of Kinshasa, the capital of Congo. Then in July 1958, a working group of prominent Belgian figures was selected to examine political developments in Congo and formulate a new policy for Congo. The working group was due to arrive in Kinshasa in October 1958. Anticipating this event, on October 10, a group of prominent Congolese, including Patrice Lumumba, Cyrille Adoula, Joseph Ileo, Arthur Pinzi, Gaston Diomi, Joseph Ngalula and Alphonse Nguvulu, sent a respectful but firm memorandum to the minister of Congo, Léon Pétillon. They demanded full independence and requested the inclusion of representative Congolese leaders in the working group. Although drawn from many ethnic groups, they presented themselves as the "Congolese National Movement" (MNC). This marked the first official act of this multi-ethnic political party. Originally, the MNC had been conceived as a temporary committee dealing only with the issue of the working group, but Lumumba succeeded in transforming the MNC into a real political party with himself as president.

The impact of the Pan-African Conferences on Lumumba's political consciousness is difficult to measure, but to some extent very real. The first pan-African conference was held in Accra, Ghana, in December 1958. He was the head of the Congolese delegation. There, he was impressed by the notion of African solidarity when he first met Kwame Nkrumah and other African nationalist leaders who had already won their countries' independence or were actively and violently fighting for it. All participants were impressed by Lumumba's eloquence, energy and belief in the pan-African ideal. He constantly emphasized that because of the central position of Congo on the African continent, its struggle for freedom was not that of a single country, but that of the entire continent. The Pan-African conferences gave Lumumba and other Congolese leaders a new sense of unity, purpose and dignity. Upon his return to Kinshasa, Lumumba sought to mobilize all segments of the Congolese population to join the struggle for independence and pan-African struggle through MNC. On Sunday, December 28, 1958, he organized a very successful rally in Kinshasa to report to the nation on the results of the Accra conference. Several thousand people attended the rally, where they heard Lumumba call for full and genuine independence. This was the first time this type of speech has been given in Congo. This demonstration was one of the triggers that led to serious riots in the capital on January 4 and 5, 1959, which in turn triggered the process that would lead Congo to an exceptionally rapid decolonization.

These riots broke out on the evening of January 4, when an ABAKO demonstration was called off because the police had not given permission. But the main political cause had been the slow progress toward autonomy, which the Congolese felt was being deliberately delayed while it was being accelerated in other parts of the continent. Thus, political events in neighbouring territories and foreign propaganda had acted as accelerating factors. The most important of these had been the promise of independence for French Equatorial Africa and the directives given at the Accra conference. The revolt in Kinshasa was entirely spontaneous, the urban masses taking their own initiative to make the slogan "immediate independence" a reality. The entire course of Congo's history was changed by their action. But two days later, on January 6, the situation was back to normal. The total number of victims was officially 49 Congolese killed and 290 wounded, including 49 Belgians; reliable estimates put the number at 1,500 Congolese killed. In addition, the Kisangani incidents took place in the context of a pro-independence demonstration following Lumumba's MNC party congress, held from October 23 to 28, 1959. The violence, which was comparable in severity to the events in Kinshasa, resulted in more than twenty deaths and the arrest of Lumumba, who was sent to the notorious underground prison in Likasi. His detention made him a very popular figure and a rallying point for the struggle for independence.

Nevertheless, the movement towards independence seemed to have become irreversible. Therefore, in a message broadcast on January 13, 1959, only a few days after the riots in Kinshasa on January 4, 1959, King Baudouin announced that Congo would be led towards independence. From that date on, progress was rapid, perhaps even precipitous.

ETHNIC LINES IN THE CONGOLESE POLITICAL ORGANISATIONS

Ethnicity, the concept of identity based on ethnic grouping, is as much a product of the European tendency to classify groups of people on the basis of their most discernible traits such as physical appearance, language, religious practices, etc, as it is a product of natural human tendency to parochialism and to value family and ancestors. But ethnic distinctions among the Congolese have always been fluid: the concept of who was or was not a member of a specific ethnic group was never as rigid as the Belgians believed. Yet the Belgian administration acted as if rigid distinctions existed. The identity cards of the Congolese mentioned the ethnic group to which they belonged, and they were required to provide this information when filling out forms. Belgium's emphasis on ethnic identity helped to reinforce the concept of ethnic identity among the Congolese. In fact, ethnicity was used by Belgian colonial authorities to divide the population of Congo and prevent the rise of a nationalist movement. It has also been used by most Congolese leaders to create power bases for their political movements.

During the colonial period, the process of urbanization led to migration from rural areas to the cities. Many people migrated to the cities in search of work and a better life, some to study. Once in the cities, they came into contact with people with whom they shared cultural characteristics, and with completely different peoples. In order to promote their culture and to support each other when competing with other ethnic groups for social and political status, these people formed ethnically based associations. Indeed, the main purpose of these various ethnic-based voluntary associations was to integrate the newcomers into the potentially hostile urban environment and to assist in the psychological adjustment of the migrant by recreating in the new urban context many of the values and conditions that were familiar to him in his rural homeland. The first association to be created was ABAKO (Bakongo Association) in 1950, then, later, the brotherhood of Lulua, the BALUBAKAT (Baluba of Katanga), the CONAKAT (Confederation of Tribal Associations of Katanga), association of Bayanzi, Kabare tribe, Union of Mongo, the tribal alliance of Banyangala, etc.

These ethnic organizations have certainly reinforced ethnic lines between groups. Some were simply based on a clear need to form an affinity group. Meanwhile, these ethnic associations, among the many forms of voluntary societies, have been at the heart of the manifestation of host institutions assisting in the adaptation and integration of the individual. In some ways, they were important in insulating the newcomer against the shock of total immersion in culturally heterogeneous urban life, providing an easily identifiable group of people who spoke the same language, shared the same attitudes, opportunities for friendship with co-ethnics, and organizing sporting events and other activities that reduced the stress of adjustment for newcomers. But even so, they had negative repercussions in terms of delaying the development of a broader and more cohesive sense of political community. The potential for inter-ethnic conflict was also exacerbated by other forms of ethnic stereotyping based on occupational monopolies enjoyed by certain groups, on assumed personality characteristics (aggressiveness, competitiveness or exclusiveness), on educational attainment, etc.

In response to growing pressure for Congolese participation in the political process, the Belgian government decreed the reorganization of the major Congolese urban centers on March 26, 1957. These first municipal elections offered a real opportunity for political organization. The speed with which this political organization had to be achieved implied a rapid mobilization of the population. There was no time to win over a large number of people through a political philosophy or ideology. The most natural way to mobilize them was through already existing ethnic organizations. The result was the formation of many political parties based primarily on ethnic loyalties. This created innumerable difficulties for Lumumba and his friends who tried to build a national political organization that could overcome ethnicity or regionalism.

Patrice Lumumba was a member of the small Tetela tribe, a Bantou-speaking group living between Lusambo and the upper Congo River in the Sankuru district of Kasai and Maniema Provinces. Ethnologists consider the Tetela and Kusu to be closely related to each other and distant members of the Mongo group. The Tetela began to be considered a separate group in the late 1800s with the arrival of Afro-Arabs from the east and Europeans from the west and south. The Tetela, living in Kasai, had less contact with Afro-Arabs than the Kusu, who in some cases adopted the Muslim religion and dress. Belgian colonial authorities separated the two groups when they divided the region into the provinces of Kasai and Kivu. Later, Patrice Lumumba sought to organize the group as a whole, but their different experiences and the orientation of the savannah Tetela towards the politics of Kasai province and the forest Tetela (Kusu) towards that of Kivu province were obstacles to true solidarity. His two main rivals, Moise Tshombe, who led the unsuccessful Katanga secession movement and became Prime Minister of Congo in 1964, and Joseph Kasavubu, who became the first President of Congo, were both from large and powerful Lunda and Kongo tribes from which they drew their main support, giving their political movements a regional character.

In Tsombe's Katanga, as elsewhere in Congo, communal elections were held in December 1957 on the subject of constitutional reform concerning the status of cities. In the capital of Katanga, Lubumbashi, these elections gave three of the four posts of burgomaster to the Luba, originally from Kasai. This victory of the "foreigners" was not well accepted by the "real Katangese" and provoked a movement of solidarity between the ethnic groups of Katanga. In order to deal with the rise of Katangese professional and social elements, Moise Tshombe and his colleagues created CONAKAT (Confederation of Tribal Associations of Katanga) in October 1958. The main goal of CONAKAT then became the repatriation of Luba "foreigners" to Kasai province.

In Kinshasa, the Bakongo, who thought they had always been the first Congolese group, felt threatened by the influx of people from far up the river, the Ngala. To counterbalance the growing influence of the Ngala in Kinshasa, they formed the ABAKO (Alliance of the Kongo people) in 1950. In addition to preserving or promoting the interests of their own ethnic group, they were concerned with the goal of inclusion in the ruling elite. At times, its leaders also advocated recreating the ancient Kongo kingdom by combining parts of Congo-Kinshasa, Angola and Congo-Brazzaville. ABAKO drew most of its strength from Bas-Congo province. However, the relatively large numbers of

Bakongo living in the capital Kinshasa added to its influence. On March 21, 1954, Joseph Kasavubu was elected president of ABAKO.

In contrast, Lumumba's movement, the MNC (National Congolese Movement), emphasized its Congolese nature and was the only political party that tried not to base itself on ethnic characteristics. It tried to develop a convincing ideology and sought to establish a nationalist program of economic, political and cultural development. The MNC was formed in October 1958 in Kinshasa by an influential group of "évolués" who had petitioned the minister of Congo with the first public demand for a comprehensive program of political change. This group wanted to form a party without ethnic orientation. The first executive committee of the party included men who would become important players in Congolese politics. After lengthy discussions, Patrice Lumumba was named president of the party. Albert Nkuli was deputy secretary general and Joseph Mbungu was treasurer. Among the members were Joseph Ileo, Joseph Ngalula, Alphonse Nguvulu, Gabriel Makoso, Maximilien Liongo, Arthur Pinzi, Gaston Diomi, Cyrille Adoula and Albert Kalonji.

As president of MNC, Lumumba established himself as one of the most dynamic and effective Congolese political organizers and orators. But his growing radicalism, independence and notoriety caused conflicts with other MNC leaders. Ethnic differences also troubled the party, which sought to gain a national constituency. Then, in 1959, with the help of colonial Belgians trying to influence the course of Congolese politics, a split occurred within the movement. On July16, 1959, the central committee of MNC published a letter from Albert Kalonji, president of the provincial section of Kasai, which he increasingly transformed into a Baluba tribal association, contrary to the movement's unitary objective. He demanded that the leadership of the movement be changed, as the MNC was becoming more and more a one-man show. The central committee decided, without consulting Lumumba, to remove him as president and to establish a collective leadership instead. This decision was taken by men protected by the church (Joseph Ileo, Joseph Ngalula, Albert Kalonji and Joseph Malula). As a result, the party was divided into two: MNC-Lumumba and MNC-Kalonji. After causing a split in the MNC, the anti-Lumumba forces created a new movement, bringing together in a kind of federation a number of political groups whose behaviour and attitudes were based on strong loyalty to their tribes, whose stated sympathies were for Christianity, federalism and anti-communism. Lumumba envisaged a dynamic unity which would not prevent considerable decentralisation in administration and even in economic affairs.

But the limited opportunities for Congolese leaders to "Africanize" the country before independence, the illegitimacy of the colonial state among the Congolese masses, and its inability to promote a sense of common national identity among the diverse peoples living within the borders of the colony are important features of the colonial legacy. For the Congolese masses, the colonial state was a foreign institution that operated according to rules and norms that were unfamiliar to them. In the same territory, the administration brought together many different ethnic groups who were forced to coexist and live according to the rules of the colonizers, who did little or nothing to promote nationalist sentiments. On the contrary, they preferred to keep the different groups apart and prevent any alliance that could be used to challenge their power. All of these elements have contributed to the political instability and fragility of Congo since independence.

CHAPTER II

POLITICAL DEVELOPMENTS DUE TO ROUND TABLE CONFERENCE

WHEN THE BELGIAN AUTHORITIES REALIZED that it was impossible to impose an independence plan on Congo, the government organized a Round Table Conference where Belgians and Congolese could determine the future of the country together. At this Round Table conference, held in Brussels from January 20 to February 20, 1960, the participants agreed to grant the Belgian Congo full independence as of June 30, 1960. This decision and the preparation of the necessary constitutional arrangements by the conference followed the decision of the Belgian Government to accelerate considerably the programme for the independence of Congo which had been announced by August de Schryver (Minister for Congo) on October 16, 1959. No final decision was taken on a number of issues arising from the achievement of independence, including the headship of the new State, its possible future special relationship with Belgium, arrangements to ensure its economic stability and the position of Belgian military bases on the territory.

Belgium was represented by August de Schryver (assisted, if necessary, by other ministers) and by 10 deputies from the Christian Social, Liberal and Socialist parties. The Congolese delegates numbered 44, of whom 11 represented the "cartel of nationalist parties", led by Kasavubu and composed of the ABAKO, the MNC-Kalonji, the PSA, the Alliance of the Bayanzi, and the General Federation of the Haut-Katanga; 11 others represented the PNP; 6 represented the parties in Katanga province; 3 from the MNC-Lumumba; and 13 from a number of small groups representing tribal or local interests. However, the highlights of the conference were: Lumumba's release from prison. His trial for incitement to violence before the Kisangani riots of October 1959 was held in Kisangani from January 18 to 21, 1960. He was convicted and sentenced to six months in prison. On January 21, representatives of the Lumumba faction of the MNC left the Brussels conference in protest. However, they returned the next day, stating that they had received assurances that Lumumba would soon arrive in Brussels. Lumumba's provisional release was announced on January

25, and he left for Brussels the same day and took his place at the conference on January 27; Kasavubu's withdrawal from the conference on January 25, after his request to give the conference the powers of a constituent assembly was rejected by de Schryver, who noted that the draft agenda, which contained no such request, had been drawn up by the heads of all Congolese delegations, including Kasavubu himself. On January 30, the cartel elected Alphonse Nguvulu (People's Party) as its president, replacing Kasavubu; Agreement on June 30,1960, when Congo would become independent. The date chosen represented a compromise between June 1 (proposed by the Congolese) and July 15 (favoured by the Belgian Government); The creation, on February 1, of two conference commissions composed of Belgian and Congolese representatives, charged with studying in detail the arrangements necessary for the establishment of the independent State.

The first Congolese Government would be formed as soon as possible after the elections were held, without waiting until June 30. The government, which must include at least one member from each province, would be constituted by King Baudouin of Belgium, who, once the election results were known and after consulting the main political parties and leaders, would appoint the person who would form the Government. This person would submit to the King the names of ministers likely to win the confident of Parliament. The Council of Ministers, headed by a Prime Minister, would be responsible to both houses of Parliament for all matters of general policy. The Prime Minister's tasks would include: the conduct of state policy in agreement with the Council of Ministers; the control and conduct of Government activity; the submission to the Head of State of proposals relating to the exercise of statutory powers and the application of laws. The Congolese Government would replace the Belgian Government on June 30, 1960, and the Belgian and Congolese Governments would agree on the manner in which mutual representation facilities would be provided. Under the fundamental law (basic law), the head of state would have powers that would include the power to issue regulations and decrees necessary for the enforcement of laws, but he could not suspend the laws themselves or grant exemptions for their enforcement. Before June 30, 1960, the two chambers of the Congolese parliament would meet in a constituent assembly to decide on the appointment of a head of state. In the event of disagreement between the Chambers, the office of head of state would be temporarily held by either the president of the House of Representatives or the president of the Senate (no final agreement has been reached on this point).

The basic law would also provide for a division of powers between the central government and the provinces. A provincial government would also be established by June 30, consisting of a president and 5 to 10 members elected by the respective provincial assembly from among its own members or from outside. A delegate of the central government would assume the direction of state services in each province. But, this basic law, which established the political institutions, was largely influenced by the Belgian political system. It provided for a bicameral parliamentary system that significantly diluted executive powers and left the division of powers between the president and prime minister unclear. This deficiency, combined with rising interregional and interethnic tensions, contributed to the political crisis that followed independence. In any case, the purpose of the system was to provide checks and balances, and to prevent abuse. However, it led to confusion and a series of confrontations between the president and the prime minister. As a result, the authority of the central government collapsed.

After the Round Table conference, a Belgian-Congolese economic conference was held in Brussels from April 26 to May 16, 1960. During most of the conference, the Congolese delegation did not include the most prominent political figures, with the exception of Moise Tshombe, the leader of CONAKAT. In the final phase, however, five Congolese members of the Executive College participated, only Lumumba refused to come to Brussels, offered his resignation from the College (which was refused), demanded the immediate recall of the troop reinforcements sent to Congo, denounced the appointment of Van der Meersch as Belgian minister for general affairs in Congo instead of the immediate establishment of a provisional government, and declared that he would boycott the meetings of the Executive College. The conclusions of the conference were welcomed by the Minister for Economic and financial Affairs of the Belgian Congo, Raymond Scheyven, on behalf of the Belgian Government. Kashamura (a member of the Congolese Executive College), however, declared on his return to Congo that neither he nor Kasavubu had formally endorsed the recommendations. Other Congolese delegates had previously stated that their purpose at the conference was only "to make an inventory".

While all of major Congolese leaders participated in the political Round Table Conference, Moise Tshombe was the only prominent politician to attend the economic Round Table Conference. It was truly a mistake to neglect to protect the country's economic assets, because it was in this last forum that the Belgians sealed the country's fate. By negotiating with university students and other politically insignificant delegates who relied on Belgian experts to understand the complex issues at stake, the Belgians laid the groundwork for the transfer of much of the huge state holdings of the colonial companies to Belgium through privatization, while leaving almost all the public debt to the new state. But if one takes into account the precipitous nature of the independence of Congo and considers that the Economic Round Table Conference was held in Brussels from April 26 to May 16, 1960, almost at the same time as the elections for the House of Representatives which took place from May 11 to 22 May, 1960, it is difficult to believe in a simple coincidence. One can naturally come to the conclusion that perhaps all this was planned by the Belgian authorities who knew full well that the Congolese leaders were more interested in themselves than in the future of Congo and would rather prefer to stay in Congo to conduct the electoral campaign because these elections meant everything to them. Thus, one can easily think that they found themselves trapped with a choice to make: stay in Congo and win the elections or participate in the Economic Round Table and lose the elections. Almost all of them stayed in Congo, leaving a free hand to the Belgians to dispose of huge state portfolios as they pleased during the Economic Conference.

Voting in the May 1960 elections was conducted along ethnic lines. Elections for the House of Representatives (the lower house of the future Congolese parliament) began on May 11 and continued in various parts of the country until May 22, when voting took place in the cities of Kinshasa, Lubumbashi and Kolwezi (Jadotville). At the same time, elections were held for the six provincial parliaments, which in turn subsequently elected members of the national Senate. Prior to and during the election period, unrest and violence erupted in various parts of Congo, resulting from both inter-party political rivalries and often intertwined tribal feuds. In these crucial May elections for the new Congolese parliament, with a voter turnout of 80.18%, Lumumba's party, the MNC (National Congolese Movement), campaigned throughout the country and won 23.44% of the 137 seats in the House of Representatives. As a result, the MNC-Lumumba became the largest party nationally, winning about a quarter of the seats (33 national deputies, 110 provincial councillors and 21 senators). Thus, the MNC-Lumumba and his allies took 41 seats, PNP (Parti National du Progrès) 15, PSA (Parti Solidaire Africain) 13, ABAKO (Association des Bakongo) 12, CEREA (Centre du Regroupement Africain) 10, MNC-Kalonji 8, CONAKAT 8, Balubakat 7 and others 23. The figures clearly confirmed that Lumumba's MNC had become the most powerful single party in both houses of the Congolese parliament. In the provincial parliaments, many seats were won by purely local or tribal groups, such as the CONAKAT, strongly represented in Katanga, the ABAKO in Kinshasa, and the CEREA in Kivu. However, some parties were represented in more than one provincial assembly, the most successful being the MNC-Lumumba, which was the only group to hold seats in all six provinces, including 58 of the 78 seats in the Eastern Province and one-third in Kasai.

Despite the fact that the "highest Belgian officials" tried to create a coalition of other Congolese parties to prevent Lumumba from becoming Prime Minister, the Belgian king, Baudouin, invited him to form the first Congolese cabinet, which took office on June 24, 1960, receiving votes of confidence from the Congolese Chamber of Representatives and Senate, which had been elected in the previous weeks with Joseph Kasongo as president of the Chamber of Representatives and Joseph Ileo as president of the Senate. Although at independence, the office of prime minister was supposed to be the most powerful position in the country, Lumumba made it clear that he considered that the head of state should also be the head of government on the American model, or the election of the head of state by direct popular vote, rather than by parliament. But the provisional constitution of the new Congolese state was embodied in a Belgian fundamental law that was signed by King Baudouin on June 19, 1960, after been unanimously approved by the Belgian House of Representatives and Senate. However, as Lumumba was unable to control a working majority, he had to form political alliances with other parties, such as ABAKO, to form a government. This created a difficult compromise between Lumumba and Kasavubu, who had represented opposing views within the Congolese independence movement. Thus, on the same day that Lumumba's government took office, Joseph Kasavubu was elected the first president of the new state by both houses of parliament with 159 votes against 43 for the only other candidate, Jean Bolikango, leader of the PUNA party. Bolikango's candidacy for the ceremonial presidency had originally been supported by Patrice Lumumba, but it was widely believed that this support had been withdrawn because of the entry of ABAKO into the Government.

In the politics of Congo, Patrice Lumumba symbolized the "radicals" who were committed to achieving real independence both politically and economically and proclaimed non-alignment on the international level. Joseph Kasavubu belonged to the "moderates", who enjoyed the support of the Belgians, other Western governments and politically conservative multinationals in Congo. He was educated in Roman Catholic schools and spent 11 years training for the priesthood before deciding, at the age of 28, to become first a teacher and then a civil servant. In 1953 he was one of the first seven to receive the "carte d'immatriculation" in Kinshasa; in 1954, he became president of ABAKO, which was then still a tribal association rather than a political party, and referring to the "carte d'immatriculation", he declared that in no civilized country are certificates given to distinguish the elite from the masses. ABAKO disapproved of division of the population into "strada", "évolués" and masses; and in 1956 it issued a manifesto calling for the immediate independence. After ABAKO's landslide victory in Kinshasa in the 1957 municipal elections, Kasavubu became mayor of the suburb of Dendale. He was arrested with other ABAKO leaders after unrest in the city in January 1959; he was later released and went to Belgium to take a leading part in the Round Table conference of January 1960. Until the eve of Congo's independence, Kasavubu had subscribed to the thesis of a federated Congo. However, as a head of state committed to protecting the integrity of the new Congo constitution, he became an advocate of national unity.

Federalists advocated strong regional states linked together by a moderate national government. Patrice Lumumba and his allies, such as Antoine Gizenga of the Parti Solidaire Africain (PSA), argued for a strong unitary state. In general, the agreements reached at the Round Table conference favoured the "unitarists". The Round Table conference also determined that, until independence, executive power would be exercised by the Governor General and a staff of six Congolese. Appointed to this executive college, Lumumba was given the Defence portfolio.

THE REPUBLIC OF CONGO UNDER THE LEADERSHIP OF LUMUMBA

When the Republic of Congo gained its independence, optimism and hopes for a bright future were high. It was assumed that the country would make a quick and easy transition to a representative democracy guided by democratic constitutions, multiparty systems, and other Western liberal institutions that had been put in place during the final stages of decolonization by the colonial power, and that the Republic of Congo would develop rapidly with the help of the more industrialized countries and participate fully in the world community. All the Congolese leaders had to do was to take control of the political destiny of their country. Unfortunately, however, most expectations proved unrealistic, and the optimism was short-lived. Instead, the Republic of Congo was simply transformed into "neo-colonialism".

Furthermore, because its political boundaries were artificial and most of its inhabitants were not united by a common historical experience, linguistic affinity, or cultural heritage, the Republic of Congo had a tenuous claim to nationhood. In many cases, pre-colonial political life was relatively decentralized, and the imposition of an artificial corporate identity during the colonial period did more to exacerbate ethnic and regional rivalries than to lay the foundations for the future political identity. In the end, history, geography and political realities seem to have conspired to put the nascent Congolese state under a trusteeship.

The Belgian Congo became independent on June 30, 1960 under the name of the Republic of Congo. The flag of the new state was a large yellow star and six smaller stars on a blue field, the design of which was approved by the Executive College on May 23; the same flag rejected by Lumumba, as "an emblem of colonialism". Lumumba's objection was based on its similarity to the flag of the Belgian Congo. The Republic of Congo, divided into six provinces, has an area of 2,345,525 square kilometers (905,600 square miles) and had about sixteen million inhabitants (more than eighty million in 2016); Kinshasa (Leopoldville), the capital, had about 400,000 inhabitants (more than ten million in 2016). Because of its location, the Republic of Congo was considered one of the most geopolitically strategic countries in Africa. It borders nine countries: Angola (including the enclave of Cabinda), Zambia, Tanzania, Burundi, Rwanda, Uganda, Sudan, Central African Republic, and Congo-Brazzaville. Mineral wealth contributes greatly to the country's economy. In 1959, Katanga's copper exports amounted to 284,000 tons, nearly one-third of the Congo's exports by value, and the Union Minière du Haut-Katanga (the main mining company) paid taxes and other levies equivalent to one-quarter of the country's ordinary budget. The company also produced about 60% of the world's cobalt. There are significant diamond deposits in Kasai, which in 1958 produced 16,000,000 carats, or about 60% of the world's supply of industrial diamonds; the Republic of Congo also produces uranium, manganese, gold, silver, coltan (80% of the world's reserves) and other minerals.

The accession to independence was preceded by ceremonies during the day in which the documents transferring power were signed, and speeches were made by King Baudouin, President Kasavubu and Prime Minister Lumumba. The Belgian Prime Minister, Gaston Eyskens, and the delegation of many other countries also attended the celebrations. In the Parliament building, before the signing of the declaration of independence, King Baudouin gave a speech in which he reviewed Belgium's contribution to the development of the Belgian

Congo, praising the greatness of King Leopold II, founder of the Congo Free State, the precursor of the Belgian Congo. President Joseph Kasavubu responded diplomatically with kind words and gratitude. He addressed the Belgians, thanking them for their civilizing mission in Congo and pledged that the Republic of Congo would cooperate with Belgium, which, he said, had set "an unprecedented example in the history of peaceful decolonization, by leading our people directly without transition from foreign domination to independence under full national sovereignty". Patrice Lumumba, conscious of being the leader of the people and the emerging Prime Minister, addressed the Congolese masses, exalting them for their fight for independence and dignity. He delivered a more direct speech in which, despite the presence of King Baudouin, he violently attacked the balance sheet of the Belgian administration, denouncing Belgium's policy of slavery and oppression in Congo during the 80 harsh years of colonialism. Appealing for help from all Congolese regardless of their ethnic ties, from all elected officials, regardless of their political party, and from foreign nations and peoples of good will, he promised that his administration would work to make the Republic of Congo a rich, free, and prosperous nation. This, he asserted, would be an important step towards the liberation of Africa as a whole. This speech made the king and his delegation felt uncomfortable during the festivities. They knew that with this man in power, their dream of neo-colonialism would be forgotten. At the official luncheon following the independence ceremony, however, Lumumba paid tribute to the Belgian achievement in Congo.

Patrice Lumumba stayed in power for only two months. But what power! The first days of independence were relatively peaceful, but soon after, the survival of the new state became doubtful. The Americans got involved, and the others followed as usual. With Lumumba in power, his enemies opted for destabilization. On the night of 5-6 July, the "Force Publique", the nation's military force, mutinied against its Belgian officers, especially after the provocation of General Emile Janssens, commander of the "Force Publique", who wrote on the blackboard "after independence = before independence" and declared bluntly that there would be no change due to independence for the men in uniform. He had been kept in his post by the Lumumba government. The mutineers demanded salary increases, the dismissal of all Belgian officers and promotions. At that time, no Congolese had risen above the rank of master sergeant. During this mutiny of the soldiers, the attacks were committed mainly against Belgians. If Janssens' intention in instigating the mutiny was to discredit Lumumba's leadership and eventually push him out of power, the immediate results were the panic and flight of civil servants and European settlers, which deprived the economy and the state of most of its professional and technical cadres. On July 7, most Belgians began to flee the six provinces of Congo to neighbouring territories. Later, this position was reversed by their return in full military force. Upon their return, Belgian forces defied the United Nations and ignored Security Council resolutions. On July 10, they went into action against Congolese soldiers in several locations, including Katanga province and the ports of Matadi and Boma; Belgian military action then spread to many other cities, including Kinshasa itself.

Prime Minister Lumumba was under great pressure. On July 10, he appointed master sergeant Victor Lundula Commander-in-Chief of the army, with the rank of general, and master sergeant Joseph Mobutu, Secretary of State for Defence, Chief of Staff, with the rank of colonel. The name of the army was changed to ANC (Congolese National army), and the reorganization and Africanization began. The new commanders were visiting garrisons around the country to calm the troops. For the most part, they succeeded, but the task of reorganizing the forces in the face of new challenges proved more difficult. As the situation became increasingly confused, the Congolese government appealed to the United Nations for help in protecting the Republic of Congo from foreign aggression on July 11, while on the same day Moïse Tshombe, the prime minister of Katanga, proclaimed the independence of his province Katanga.

The secession of Katanga gave rise to other secessionist movements. Later, on August 9, Albert Kalonji proclaimed the independence of a "Mining State" in the southern part of Kasai, with Joseph Ngalula as prime minister. The Abako party, Bolikango's Puna party and other tribal political parties were calling for the immediate establishment of a confederation of Congo, including a "Kongo Kingdom", a "Republic of Equator" and other "Tribal Republics". The Belgians in Lubumbashi (Katanga) played a very successful game against Tshombe, Munongo, Kibwe, Kimba and their friends who were so naive to believe that Belgium would immediately recognize the independent state of Katanga. No country in the world accorded the secessionist province the expected official recognition, not even Belgium in the cruellest blow of all. But, Tshombe's secession had international support anyway. The United States, Belgian and most Western governments openly supported the Katangese.

For Tshombe, however, the idea of a federal Congo allowing autonomy equivalent to secession for Katanga stemmed mainly from the 1959 recession and rising ethnic tensions with the Luba from Kasai. He hoped to see an autonomous state of Katanga, in order to stop the "ruinous immigration" of Luba and to keep more of the mineral profits for the Katangese whose copper came from the soil. In this regard, the rapid rise of the MNC led by Patrice Lumumba evoked the menace not only of radical foreign influence, but also of continued dominance by a government outside the province. As president of CONAKAT, Tshombe included in his coalition the Union of Katanga, an association of Belgian settlers known for their secessionist, or at least federalist, views. These Belgians wanted autonomy for different reasons than Tshombe. For them, the main threat was the radical view of Patrice Lumumba, who advocated a unitary state. They felt that their interests would be better preserved under an autonomous regime led by a moderate, who was well-disposed to their interests. Then, at the national level, Patrice Lumumba had won the leadership battle and formed a central government. Katanga was given two ministerial portfolios; Tshombe considered this share insufficient and attempted to proclaim the independence of Katanga before the Belgian Congo became independent on June 30, 1960. However, supported by the Belgian community in Katanga, the Belgian military, financiers and politicians in Belgium, Tshombe proclaimed the independence of Katanga eleven days after June 30. In reality, Tshombe served as an African front for the more powerful interests of the mining companies and white settlers. The prospect of an independent Congo ruled by a radical unitary nationalist government brought the Union of Katanga, the white settlers' association, and Moise Tshombe's CONAKAT together. The Union of Katanga helped prepare for secession. But to give it credibility in an international environment marked by overwhelming support for national self-determination, independence and majority rule, the colonists needed Congolese allies to defend them. And they found them in Moise Tshombe's CONAKAT.

On July 14, the United Nations Security Council adopted a resolution authorizing the immediate dispatch of a UN military force to the Republic of Congo, and calling on Belgium to withdraw its troops. The first UN soldiers arrived in Kinshasa on July 15, and by July 28 the force had grown to more than 10,000 with units in all provinces except Katanga. The UN military force was consisted of troops from Canada, Egypt, Ethiopia, Ghana, Guinea, India, Indonesia, Irish Republic, Liberia, Mali, Morocco, Pakistan, Sudan, Sweden, and Tunisia. The Congolese Government's reaction against Belgium was to break off diplomatic relations between the two countries. The landing of Belgian troops convinced the Congolese authorities that Belgium was attempting to reoccupy the country.

In addition to the internal disintegration and the rivalry between the many Congolese factions, the problem was further complicated by the fact that many Western European, mainly Belgian, economic and financial interests felt threatened, directly or indirectly, by the transfer of power in the republic of Congo. In addition, the real power struggle also manifested itself in the United Nations where the great powers Soviet Union, the United States, the United Kingdom and France were unable to agree on a common policy. In the West, the situation in Congo was seen in strategic terms rather than as a question of sovereignty and territorial integrity. The United States was especially concerned that Lumumba, the so-called radical, would bring this mineral-rich, strategically located central African country into the Soviet sphere of influence. As a result, Dag Hammarskjöld, the Secretary General of the United Nations, who died on September 18, 1961 in a plane crash in Africa, was caught up in the usual conflict between great powers, and Lumumba reiterated his threat to appeal to the USSR or other countries if the Security Council did not give the Republic of Congo satisfaction. Later, a communiqué issued by President Nkrumah and Prime Minister Lumumba stated that the two Heads of Government had decided, in agreement with other independent African States, that if the UN was unable to secure the immediate withdrawal of the Belgian troops from the whole of Congo, they would create a combined "High Command of military forces" to achieve this objective and would appeal to any other country prepared to provide sincere assistance in this matter. As prime minister, Lumumba did what he could to redress the situation. His army was an uncertain instrument of power, his civilian administration was untrained and unproven; the United Nations forces were condescending and assertive, and the political alliances that underpinned his regime were very fragile. The Belgian troops did not evacuate, and the secession of Katanga continued.

The period between mid-August and September was marked by a serious deterioration in relations between Lumumba and Hammarskjöld on the one hand, and by open conflict between President Kasavubu and Prime Minister Lumumba on the other. The former followed Hammarskjöld's visit to Lubumbashi, where he had discussed with Tshombe the modalities of replacing Belgian troops in Katanga with UN forces, without offering facilities to the central government to take military action against the secession of Katanga. The dispute between the two Congolese leaders followed Lumumba's attempts to suppress other secessionist movements in Kasai, Leopoldville province and Equator. Moreover, it had been suggested that Kasavubu was more acceptable to Western governments than the radical Lumumba. They wanted to establish an influential puppet regime in Kinshasa, which was not possible under Lumumba's leadership. Therefore, they promoted events that would lead to constant disorder in order to make things more difficult for the prime minister. They pushed Kasavubu to remove him from office on September 5, 1960. Lumumba and his cabinet responded by accusing the president of high treason and voted to dismiss him. The Congolese parliament confirmed both leaders in their positions, as did the African countries. While this game of rivalry was going on, the UN seized the radio station in Kinshasa, preventing Prime Minister Lumumba from using it. President Kasavubu had the advantage of being able to broadcast his programs through Radio Congo in Brazzaville (capital of French Congo).

For a time, it seemed that Nkrumah's influence on Lumumba had some effect and the prospects for peace seemed bright. But Kasavubu's insistence on removing Lumumba and Lundula, appointing Joseph Ileo as Prime Minister and Joseph Mobutu as head of the ANC, caused the crisis to erupt. This situation was further complicated when, on September 14, 1960, Mobutu announced that he would assume power until December 31,1960, to give Lumumba and Kasavubu time to reach an agreement. He set up a government of young graduates and university students (college of commissioners) to serve as a provisional government. The Commissioners, 15 in number, would not be called ministers, but one or more of them would be given responsibility for various departments of government. They had studied either in Belgium or at the University of Lovanium in Kinshasa, and almost all of them had attended the Economic Round Table conference in Brussels in April-May as technicians; they were considered to be more interested in economic than in political matters. Joseph Désiré Mobutu (later President Mobutu Sese Seko) served for seven years in the former "Force Publique" under Belgian rule, attaining the rank of master sergeant; after leaving the service in 1956, he took a course at the Institute of Social Studies in Brussels and returned to Kinshasa to begin a career as a journalist. At the same time, he was an active member of the MNC, and remained a supporter of Lumumba after the movement split in 1959 and participated in the Brussels round table conference in January 1960. When Lumumba's Government was formed in May 1960, he became Secretary of State for Defence, returned to the army as Chief of Staff after the July mutiny, then General, Field Marshal and finally President of the Democratic Republic of Congo (the Republic of Zaïre) from 1965 to 1997.

Subsequent events would show that Kasavubu and Mobutu were all on the same side against Lumumba. Since then, Kasavubu has been supported both by the UN command and, from October 1960, by elements of the Congolese army controlled by Mobutu. Kasavubu controlled the capital. Despite this, Lumumba continued to assert that he was the legal government, and some of his supporters, led by Deputy Prime Minister Antoine Gizenga, took control of the northeast of the country in November 1960. Gizenga's government operated from Kisangani. What happened in Congo affected Africa. The continent was divided into three camps: moderates, revolutionaries and neutrals. The revolutionaries supported Lumumba's forces against Kasavubu. And the moderates were behind Kasavubu.

Therefore, the future of Congo became uncertain. The political leaders responsible for the independence of Congo were deeply torn by internal contradictions due to their own weaknesses and the destabilizing actions of the Belgians. They were opportunistic in jumping on the independence bandwagon without a clear understanding of where it would lead them to, and inexperienced in failing to address the economic aspects of the transfer of power. If the end of colonial rule was a revolution in the sense that the white regime disappeared and was replaced by a black regime, it was rather a partial, purely political revolution that left the pillars of the edifice standing. Given its precipitous nature, the international context in which it took place and the crisis it provoked, the independence of Congo was also a very fragile political revolution.

THE DEATH OF A PROPHET

Having successfully removed Lumumba from office, the anti-Lumumba alliance of UN officials, Belgian authorities, American diplomats and Congolese moderates was now concerned with how to prevent him from regaining power.

Seeing that, power was slipping away, Lumumba, who had been under UN protection since his removal, decided to leave for Kisangani to take control of the ANC troops and the government. He had agreed to follow the advice of his supporters, who were pressing him, for his own safety, to join them in Kisangani where troops loyal to him had gathered. Although his house was surrounded by UN troops and by ANC (Congolese National Army) soldiers, on the evening of November 27, 1960, Lumumba managed to slip out of the house by hiding on the floor of an MNC station wagon that regularly passed by the house. With his wife, his son Roland, and several loyal politicians, Lumumba left Kinshasa by car in the direction of Kasai. They left in a large big convoy of cars, and it was Mungul Diaka, who later became Mobutu's prime minister, who was supposed to drive them through the Kasai to the Sankuru River. They took the most direct route, but Patrice Lumumba was delayed for a long time by unexpected meetings along the way. He had to make speeches.

When Lumumba's escape was reported, Kasavubu, Mobutu and Tshombe were in Brazzaville to participate in ceremonies celebrating the independence of the former French Congo. Mobutu immediately returned to Kinshasa, ordering the Army to capture him. U.S and Belgian intelligence services quickly offered their assistance to Mobutu. A Sabena helicopter was made available for this purpose. Meanwhile, the Catholic missionary in Bandundu made a radio call, informing Mobutu of Lumumba's presence. Lumumba and his companions could hear the sound of the helicopter searching for them. Lumumba left in the first pirogue to cross the Sankuru River, flanked by faithful soldiers. The pirogue could not accommodate them all, so his wife, son and driver waited for the pirogue to come back for them. When they crossed to the other side, they found soldiers waiting to arrest them. There were already traitors even in the pirogue. Although Lumumba managed to get within a few kilometers of friendly territory, he was arrested at Lodi in the Kikwit region at about 11 p.m. on December 1, 1960, while crossing the Sankuru River and sent to Kinshasa. His wife Pauline was detained for hours. After suffering further humiliation and brutal beatings at the Binza parachutist camp in the presence of Mobutu, Lumumba was transferred to the elite camp of the Ebeya armored brigade in Mbanza-Ngungu, Bas-Congo province.

Even in jail, Lumumba continued to pose a threat to moderate leaders and their Western backers. The Lumumbist government in Kisangani began to extend its control and authority in the eastern part of the Republic of the Congo and thus encouraged Lumumba's supporters throughout the country to continue the struggle for genuine independence, national unity and territorial integrity. American and Belgian officials were greatly alarmed by rumours of a pro-Lumumba coup. Moderate Congolese authorities also fear that the soldiers guarding Lumumba in Mbanza-Ngungu could release him, as he was capable of triggering an uprising among the soldiers in the camp. For Washington and Brussels, the time had come to get rid of Lumumba physically, but not without the involvement of his Congolese enemies in the conspiracy to kill him.

Finally, aware that an imprisoned Lumumba was more dangerous than a dead Prime Minister, on January 17, 1961, in what most historians consider a calculated move to eliminate him, he was transferred, along with his two companions Maurice Mpolo, Minister of Youth, and Joseph Okito, Vice President of the Senate, to the secessionist regime in Katanga. They were severely beaten during the plane trip to Katanga, in the presence of two members of the College of Commissioners, Defence Commissioner Ferdinand Kazadi and Internal Affairs Commissioner Jonas Mukamba. Then, upon their arrival in Lubumbashi, they were tortured at the Brouwez villa not far from the Luano airport, and later shot by a firing squad under the command of Belgian Captain Julien Gat. The next day, Belgian police commissioner Gerard Soete and his brother removed the bodies from the burial site, cut them into small pieces and dissolved them in 200 liters of sulphuric acid. Later, they scattered the remains of the bodies, burnt bones, belt buckles, teeth, etc. As a result, their bodies were never found.

For almost a month, the assassinations were kept secret. When Lumumba's death was announced on February 13, 1961, it led to anarchy in many areas. The Republic of Congo seemed irreversibly fragmented. There were two capitals, Kinshasa and Kisangani, each claiming to be the legitimate capital of the country. His death completely changed the course of events in the Republic of Congo. It divided the entire country and its people. An immediate result of Lumumba's death was the decision of a number of countries in Eastern Europe, Africa and Asia to recognize the regime of Antoine Gizenga (deputy prime minister in Lumumba's government) in Kisangani as the legal government of Congo. The countries that granted this recognition were the USSR, Poland, Rumania, Czechoslovakia, Bulgaria, Yugoslavia, Egypt, Ghana, Guinea, Mali, Morocco, Indonesia and Cuba. A Soviet resolution was presented in the Security Council on February 14, denouncing the murder of Lumumba, Mpolo and Okito as "an international crime incompatible with the Charter of the United Nations" and calling for Hammarskjöld's removal from the post of UN Secretary General.

Pro-Lumumba and anti-Belgian demonstrations took place from February 14 to 16 in a number of capitals in East Europe, Africa and Asia, accompanied in some cases by serious riots. The most violent scenes took place in Moscow, Cairo and Belgrade where crowds of several thousand people attacked Belgian Embassies, smashing windows and burning furniture; in retaliation, Belgian students attacked and stoned the Soviet and Egyptian Embassies in Brussels. Smaller demonstrations took place in Accra, Colombo and other cities in Africa and Asia, as well as in some Western capitals, including London, where 29 people were arrested when a crowd of 3,000 attempted to march on the Belgian Embassy in Eaton Square. In New York, shortly after the Security Council began its debate on February 15, meetings had to be suspended for half an hour due to a violent disturbance in the public galleries caused by demonstrators who shouted Lumumbist and African nationalist slogans, refused to leave the room when asked to do so, and attacked UN guards with knives and bicycle chains. Eighteen UN guards were wounded, and many demonstrators were in a state of hysteria.

Indeed, Patrice Lumumba has been the subject of debate in Africa, America, Europe and around the world. His death took away a man who, during his lifetime, always represented a challenge to those who were in power in Congo. He was loved, hated and feared. More for what he said as a statesman than for what he accomplished as a politician. As a statesman, he talked a lot, too much in fact, both in public and in private. As a politician he maneuvered skillfully to achieve his goals. His enemies and some of his so-called friends became afraid. They misinterpreted his words. They exaggerated his words, giving what he said or did, the meaning they wanted rather than the meaning he intended. It has often been said that Lumumba's impromptu speech on Independence Day in front of the Belgian King Baudouin sealed his doom. It has also been pointed out that he had offended him by giving his speech. The Belgians wanted him to respond to their king, as Kasavubu had done, with kind words and gratitude, thanking them for their civilizing mission in Congo. But didn't Belgian King Baudouin offend the Congolese on the same day with his speech in which he praised the greatness of king Leopold II, knowing full well that the latter had committed genocide in Congo? In fact, the fall and assassination of Lumumba were the result of a vast conspiracy involving the United States, Belgium, the Western Powers and UN officials on the one hand, and his Congolese political enemies, notably Kasavubu, Mobutu and Tshombe, on the other.

Lumumba's dream had always been to lead the Republic of Congo, to become the equal, and if possible, the superior of the most illustrious leaders in the history of African liberation. His immediate ambition was to be the Head of the Congolese government. A surprising fact seems to have determined Lumumba's political life: his close friends declared that he was predestined not to live long. He was convinced of his mission to liberate Congo, but he also firmly believed that he had only little time at his disposal, and that he had to do everything he could as quickly as possible. This would certainly explain his impatience, his impulsive behaviour, his mistrust of all those who advised him to wait, to give himself time, to think carefully about his actions and to think before he spoke. One day, he gathered his wife and children, and told them that he was probably going to die, that many plots had already been foiled. Somehow he knew what was going on. Not only did he feel misunderstood by his friends and countrymen, but in the end he knew he was going to die.

Lumumba often spoke of this: "I know that I will never have the chance to see my children grow up". And he said it regularly to his wife. It was towards the end and he knew what was going to happen. That is why he decided to send the older children to Egypt in November 1960. The Egyptian president Gamal Abdel Nasser invited Lumumba's entire family after the assassinations and took care of them until his death.

Now dead, Lumumba is described as a "national hero" for the Congolese people and all of Africa, and his assassination as one of the colonialists' most grievous crimes. Because, the particularity of this crime lies in the fact that it was committed under the blue flag of the United Nations. The Americans, the Belgians, their allies and their agents bear the full measure of responsibility for these crimes. Kasavubu, Mobutu and Tshombe will not escape their responsibility before the peoples of Congo and Africa for having been the puppets of the Americans and Belgians. In fact, there are three distinct levels of responsibility. At the highest level, there was a Congo committee chaired by Belgian Prime Minister Gaston Eyskens and including Belgian Minister of African Affairs Harold d'Aspremont Lynden and Belgian Minister of Foreign Affairs Pierre Wigny. The latter two orchestrated the entire assassination plan through their assistants such as Major Jules Loos, military advisor to d'Aspremont Lynden. And it was this minister who gave the final order for the transfer of Lumumba to Lubumbashi, which took place on January 17, 1961 in a Sabena DC4 plane under the command of the Belgian Captain Piet Van der Meersch. The Belgian government did not want to negotiate a compromise with Prime Minister Lumumba, as the Congolese Government had suggested. On the contrary, it took a leading role in the organization of his assassination through the intermediary of Belgian officers still in power in the Republic of Congo.

In the United States, a Senate Committee headed by Senator Frank Church investigated in 1975 the role of the Central Intelligence Agency (CIA) in the Lumumba's assassination. After documenting everything the Agency did to plan and assist Lumumba's political rivals in the Republic of Congo to kill him, the commission absolved the CIA, since it did not actually carry out the act of assassination. But testifying before the U.S senate committee, Lawrence Devlin, who was the CIA station chief in Kinshasa in the 1960s, admitted that the CIA had a plan to assassinate Patrice Lumumba and had even made initial preparations to carry it out. But he said, the plan was never carried out. He admitted that, although he had no moral objection to the principle of political assassination when circumstances required it, the killing of Lumumba was never a measure that he personally considered necessary or intended to carry out. He hoped that the Congolese would settle the matter among themselves, one way or another. But perhaps, Devlin just sanitized his account with the passage of time. He knew very well that the elimination and assassination of Lumumba was an urgent and overriding goal of the CIA, and he helped Lumumba's enemies to achieve that goal. The authorisation came from President Eisenhower himself. Although it appears that the CIA did not directly assassinate Lumumba, it was, at the very least, present behind the scenes to encourage and facilitate it. The evidence leaves little doubt that American officials encouraged Lumumba's opponents to eliminate him. Specifically, there is also evidence that Devlin had something to do with the organization of Lumumba's transfer to Katanga and that the CIA subsequently took credit for the assassination.

In Belgium, new revelations by Ludo De Witte, a Belgian sociologist, about the role of Belgian authorities in the assassination forced the government to approve, in December 1999, the creation of a parliamentary commission of inquiry. Finally, on February 5, 2002, Belgium presented its official "regrets" and "apologies" for its role in the assassination of the first Prime Minister of Congo Patrice Lumumba, and his two companions Maurice Mpolo and Joseph Okito. By admitting that "certain Belgian actors bear an irrefutable responsibility for the events that led to Lumumba's death", Louis Michel, the Belgian foreign minister, went one step further than the Lumumba commission itself, which had only admitted Belgian "moral responsibility" in the assassination. I do not understand why the Belgian government has still not admitted that it played a key role in the assassination of Lumumba. There is clear evidence that no one can deny: The Sabena DC4 plane in which Lumumba was transferred to Lubumbashi was under the command of Belgian Captain Piet Van der Meersch; Lumumba and his two companions were shot by a firing squad under the command of Belgian Captain Julien Gat; Belgian police commissioner Gerard Soete was in charge of removing the bodies from the burial site, cutting them into small pieces and dissolving them in sulfuric acid. Claude Grandelet, a Belgian officer, one of the witnesses of the last hours of the mythical figure of the Congolese independence, tells that he is sent urgently to the airport of Luano. He took a seat in the turret of an armoured car driven by the Belgian brigadier Francois Son. Three prisoners were unloaded from the DC4 plane, including Patrice Lumumba, the Congolese Prime Minister who had been held since December in the military camp of Thysville (Mbanza-Ngungu) in Bas-Congo. They were dragged to a jeep under ranting and blows of sticks. Perched in the turret of his armoured car, Lieutenant Grandelet followed the convoy that took the prisoners to the Brouwez house, the requisitioned villa of a Belgian settler. On the spot, the prisoners were brutalized by the soldiers in charge of guarding them. Grandelet asked to see Lumumba. The Belgian captain Julien Gat, who had the key to the bathroom where he had locked up Lumumba, accompanied him. No one could go there without his authorization. Grandelet saw Lumumba sitting by the toilet, knees bent, hands tied behind his back. He was marked by the blows he had received, but had no open wounds and was conscious. Part of his hair had been torn off and he no longer had glasses. For Claude Grandelet, Patrice Lumumba appeared very dignified. He knew that everything was over for him.

Any sensible person can come to the conclusion that if "certain Belgian actors bear an irrefutable responsibility for Lumumba's death, as the Belgian Minister of Foreign Affairs, Louis Michel, admitted in February 2002", but these "certain Belgian actors" could never have acted alone if the authorization had not come from the top of the Belgian State. The Belgians cannot lie to themselves and think they can hide the truth from the Congolese people all the time. Therefore, with the benefit of hindsight, I understand better today the reaction of my son, Preston Paul Nzinga Mumbata. Even though he was only 15 years old in 2012, as we travelled by bus from Denmark to France through Belgium, he refused to let his feet touch Belgian soil when the bus stopped there for a while. I tried every way to convince him otherwise, but to no avail. He, who was born in Denmark, could not understand why his father, who was born in Congo, was comfortable in Belgium, a country that committed genocide through its King Leopold II by killing millions of Congolese during colonization and then committed one of the most serious crimes of the colonialists by assassinating Prime Minister Patrice Emery Lumumba. And all this only because Belgium wanted to own Congo, which is one of the richest countries in the world, if not the richest in terms of natural resources. My son, Preston Mumbata, has argued that the Congolese people must honour all these dead in the same way that the Jews and other peoples of the world do when genocide occurs. It is an indispensable duty of memory. And he added that if the situation was reversed, how would the Belgians have reacted if their King Baudouin had been assassinated by the Congolese and one of his teeth had been kept by his executioner? It is clear that the Democratic Republic of Congo would have paid for this crime to this day.

In any case, Lumumba's wife, Pauline Opango now deceased, did not have the opportunity to testify and tell "her truth" to the Lumumba Commission because the family appointed Francois Lumumba (the eldest son) as its representative. But she was in Belgium to hear it from the Belgian Minister of Foreign Affairs. While she was watching Louis Michel live on television, the text of the famous letter that Lumumba, arrested and beaten mercilessly by his jailers, had written to her in early January 1961, in which he prophesied that "history will one day have its say, but it will not be the history that is taught in Brussels...Africa will write its own history, and north and south of the Sahara, it will be a glorious and dignified history", must have floated over Pauline's misty eyes.

This letter deserves to be quoted in its entirety:

"My dear wife", Lumumba began.

"I write these words without knowing if they will reach you, when they will reach and if I will still be alive when you read them.

Throughout my struggle for the independence of my country, I have never doubted for a single instant the final triumph of the sacred cause to which my companions and I have dedicated our entire lives.

But what we wished for our country, its right to an honourable life, to unstained dignity, to independence without restrictions, was never desired by the Belgian imperialists and their Western allies who found direct and indirect support, both deliberate and unintentional amongst certain high officials of the United Nations, this organization in which we placed all our trust when we called for its assistance.

They have corrupted some of our compatriots and bribed others. They have contributed to distorting the truth and dishonouring our independence. How can I speak otherwise? Dead or alive, free or in prison by order of the imperialists, it is not me who counts, it is Congo. It is our poor people for whom independence has become a cage on the other side of which the outside world looks at us, sometimes with deep sympathy, sometimes with joy and pleasure.

But my faith will remain unshaken. I know and I feel in my heart that sooner or later my people will get rid of all their enemies, internal and external, and that they will stand up as one man to say no to the degradation and shame of colonialism, and will regain their dignity in the clear light of the sun.

We are not alone. Africa, Asia and the free and liberated peoples of the world will always stand by the millions of Congolese who will not give up the struggle until the day when there will be no more colonizers and mercenaries on our soil. As for my children, whom I am leaving and whom I may never see again, I would like them to know that Congo has a great future, and that it is up to them, as it is up to every Congolese, to accomplish the sacred task of rebuilding our independence and our sovereignty; because without dignity, there is no freedom, without justice, there is no dignity, and without independence, there are no free men.

Neither brutality, nor cruelty, nor torture will ever bring me to ask for mercy, for I would rather die with my head held high, my faith unshaken, and my deep trust in the destiny of my country, than to live submissively and in defiance of sacred principles.

History will one day have its say, but it will not be the history taught in Brussels, Paris, Washington or the United Nations, but the history that will be taught in the countries liberated from imperialism and its puppets. Africa will write its own history, and north and south of the Sahara, it will be a glorious and dignified history.

Do not weep for me, my dear wife, I know that my country, which is suffering so much, will be able to defend its independence and its freedom.

Long live Congo. Long live Africa!"

What a man of dignity was Lumumba! Knowing that he was going to be killed, he refused to ask for mercy and to ignore the sacred principles. He was truly a man of strong character who intended to pursue his politics, no matter what enemies he made within his country or abroad. Moreover, the Republic of Congo was a key area in terms of geopolitics of Africa, and because of its wealth, size and contiguity with White-dominated southern Africa, Lumumba's opponents had reason to fear the consequences of a radical or radicalized Congolese regime. Moreover, in the context of the Cold War, the Soviet Union's support for Lumumba appeared at the time to be a threat to many in the West, and the cynicism of the Western powers became even more evident once the main threat to their interests in Congo had been eliminated. After Lumumba's assassination and the elimination of his friends and supporters from the political scene in Kinshasa, the United States, Belgium and other Western Powers decided they could do profitable business in the Congo with the pro-Western moderates they had helped put in power.

CHAPTER III

CHARISMA AND BEHAVIOUR OF THE ELITE

ALL OVER THE WORLD, PEOPLE tend to look to their leaders as role models. The mimicry of leaders' behavior, including their gestures, is eloquent proof of this. In Congo, Lumumba was an example. Because he sported a goatee and parted his hair, thousands of people followed his example. During Lumumba's short tenure as a national leader, many events made him a hero in the public eye. Congolese artists took advantage of these events to exercise their creative spirit. In many ways, they portrayed Lumumba as an extraordinary human being, unique among Congolese leaders in his courage, power and dedication to the liberation of the Republic of Congo. For example, many artists portrayed him with the Congolese delegation at the Round Table Conference in Brussels to discuss the independence of Congo.

And on the eve of the independence, Congolese leaders created political parties, most of which had an ethnic base. Patrice Lumumba's party, the MNC, was practically the only truly nationalist political party. Kinshasa and Kisangani were the party's main strongholds, but it also had representatives elsewhere. One of the manifestations of political life, after the creation of political parties and the Round Table Conference, was the electoral campaign. In one scene, Lumumba is shown carrying signs that read: "Everybody votes for MNC". In another, he is shown holding an election campaign meeting in a village, standing with his arms in the air, surrounded by men and women. Some paintings depicting the events of Independence Day show Prime Minister Lumumba, King Baudouin and President Kasavubu addressing dignitaries and the public. Patrice Lumumba is certainly the most glorified hero to date in the Democratic Republic of Congo.

Indeed, a considerable amount of information has been published, since his death, especially concerning his relation with Congolese political leaders, the Belgians and members of his family. Using social distance as a criterion, two groups of officials can be identified: his close friends considered as radicals and other leaders called moderates. Lumumba's relationship with his close friends was between equals, despite the fact that his close friends were willing to satisfy his every wish. Their long years as members of the club of "évolués", members of APIC, members of MNC, and later members of the government had the effect of minimizing the social distance between them. It is clear that this relationship was not one of dominance. Having established the charismatic bond and experienced mass adulation, Lumumba did not treat his close friends as expendable errand boys.

In reality, Lumumba himself had not changed, but his friends had changed their opinion of him. Some wanted the privilege of publicly proclaiming themselves his close friends, others saw themselves as benefactors to whom Lumumba owed some gratitude. Nevertheless, both groups were proud of this former postal worker turned Prime Minister. And he, while remaining affable with his former friends, white or black, could never forget his new status and responsibilities. But there is no reliable information as to whether the reaction of some of his close friends was one of bitterness and jealousy towards a colleague who had been elevated above the group by the force of charisma. It can be seen that during the Congo crisis, they formed a kind of bloc behind Lumumba. They supported him against the others in all his decisions. After his assassination, they felt even closer to him. In his name, they rebelled against all the central governments formed in Kinshasa. Most of them were killed defending Lumumba's cause and the rights of the Congolese to full independence.

Lumumba's relationship with moderate leaders was based on respect. Even though their views on the political direction of Congo were opposed to his own, he managed to establish a fairly friendly relationship with them, especially with Kasavubu, as they were working together for the development of Congo. It was later with the Congo crisis and the help of Western powers that Kasavubu and his friends began to consider Lumumba as their enemy. Lumumba himself stated that he had always considered Kasavubu as one of his friends. He had never felt antagonism towards him. If Kasavubu was head of state, it was because of him. Lumumba used his parliamentary majority in favour of Kasavubu rather than Bolikango, the other candidate. He himself said that he did not want to be head of state because he was still too young (35 years old) and preferred to work, as the office of prime minister was supposed to be the most powerful. The office of head of state was only a ceremonial presidency. He knew that even some members of the opposition did not want Kasavubu to be elected, because he was seen as a separatist; they preferred Bolikango.

When a split developed within the MNC in 1959 and grew into a firm schism, with one wing of the party known as the MNC Lumumba, and the other wing as the MNC Kalonji, Lumumba nevertheless continued to cooperate with Kalonji on certain issues. Albert Kalonji became increasingly identified with the group of politicians who advocated federation along ethnic lines. Lumumba, on the other hand, continued to insist on a unitary government, regardless of ethnic differences. Federalism, in his view, was only a subterfuge for separatism and division. Despite their differences, however, Lumumba campaigned for Kalonji's release when he was placed under house arrest in 1959.

However, the events of July and September 1960 changed Lumumba's relationship with some of his ministers and colleagues. He seemed to fight a very lonely battle. When things were going well, he was surrounded by friends and admirers, some of whom were false and even actively conspired against him. But at the first sign of trouble, he found himself alone and struggling alone. Joseph Mobutu, his close friend, whom he had appointed personal secretary of the MNC, then secretary of state in the government, and finally chief of staff of the Congolese army, betrayed him to the Kasavubu group. Later, both Kasavubu and Mobutu played a key role in the assassination of Lumumba.

Lumumba's family knew Mobutu very well. He met Patrice Lumumba when he was studying journalism in Brussels. The two men shared many of the same instincts: a belief in a strong, united Congo and resentment of foreign interference. Through Lumumba's influence, Mobutu would become a full member of the MNC. He acted as Lumumba's trusted personal assistant, deciding who he saw, scheduling his activities. He really felt at home in Lumumba's house. He came and went as he pleased, and helped himself to whisky and beer. He spent his days there. He was totally immersed in the family life of Lumumba. Patrice Lumumba used to trust people quite easily and quickly. He was a good man. He used to tell his wife that Mobutu was his friend and that he was welcome in their house. Lumumba knew very well that Mobutu needed money to help his family, but he advised him not to betray the Republic of Congo and its people for that. But Mobutu, like Judas Iscariot betrayed Jesus-Christ by going to the chief priests, betrayed his own friend by going to the Belgians and Americans.

Patrice Lumumba made a serious mistake by relying on his excessive confidence in the loyalty of the people around him. Although he was a very intelligent, quick-witted man with considerable power over the common people, he was very passionate and lacked pragmatism. These characteristics clouded his intelligence, in that he made many errors of thought, judgment and moderation. He refused to listen to the apparently well-founded rumours about Mobutu's links with Belgian and American intelligence services when he appointed him colonel and chief of the staff of the ANC. Despite what his friends said, Lumumba kept Mobutu close to him. He had unwittingly chosen his own Judas.

Lumumba respected and appreciated the Belgian King Baudouin. They spoke for a long time in Kisangani, when the King visited the Congo for the first time in 1955. For Lumumba, who became Prime Minister, the future of Congo had to be built with the support of the Belgians, among others. He repeatedly said that they were welcome in the Republic of Congo, and when he could, he defended and protected them. His best friends were Belgian, like Jean Van Lierde, who was one of his confidential and close friends. But Lumumba himself did not know why the Belgians hated him so much. He only wanted the Congolese people to have a better life and a better access to education.

Lumumba's relationship with his family was based on love and respect. His wife Pauline Opango was born in Katako-Kombe like him. They had three children, Patrice, Juliana and Roland. During the crisis that preceded her husband's assassination, while the family was still under house arrest in Kinshasa, Pauline was so stressed that she gave birth to a premature baby girl, Marie Christine, who died a few days later. But Lumumba had another son, Francois, with his first wife who was also named Pauline. His wife describes the man she knew around 1950 in Kisangani, when he was working at the post office, as a "good husband and father" who protected her. He was kind, and whenever he could, he played with the children in the garden. But he was always reading and studying because he had to learn a lot by himself. He often did not speak for long hours.

Patrice Lumumba was able to express himself easily in french, swahili (the language spoken in Eastern Congo) and lingala (the language spoken by most Congolese). He became a powerful charismatic figure who could move the Congolese and the African masses with his message of African unity. He was so well known for his political eloquence that in December 1958, a Kinshasa hotel clerk took East African leaders A.R. Mohamed Babu and Tom Mboya, who had stopped in Kinshasa on their way to the Pan-African Conferences in Accra, Ghana, to meet him. They were so impressed with Lumumba that they sought and obtained financial resources from home to bring him to Accra with two other Congolese leaders, Gaston Diomi and Joseph Ngalula. There, Lumumba met Kwame Nkrumah, Gamal Abdul Nasser and many other leaders who would later support him in his struggle to defend the independence and territorial integrity of Congo. Kwame Nkrumah, Gamal Nasser and Patrice

Lumumba were very much in favour of the idea of creating a United States of Africa with a political, economic and monetary union.

It was from Accra Conference that Lumumba brought back to Congo new political perspectives, a mature nationalism and a strong commitment to the African national project. The main components of this project, which continue to define Lumumbism as a political ideology and a heroic legacy in the Democratic Republic of Congo, are national unity, economic independence and pan-African solidarity. He was provided with extraordinary energy and ambition. His political power extended to neighbouring Congo-Brazzaville. In one of his famous speeches during the struggle for independence, he declared that the two Congo were one nation. He therefore praised the unification of the two countries.

In the Congolese political mosaic, Lumumba symbolized the Congolese collective quest for greatness. He could address the Congolese Parliament in a spiritual way, which Kasavubu, the President, could not hope to accomplish. If his personal charisma legitimized the struggle for independence, it also placed him above all other Congolese leaders. But Patrice Emery Lumumba was an idealist, and like all pure and sincere idealists, he often lacked realism; too often he thought that wanting something was as good as having it already, and that conceiving an original idea was as good as implementing it.

THE ROLE OF POLITICAL PROPAGANDA IN CONGO

MASS MEDIA ARE COMMUNICATION METHODS designed to reach a wide audience. In ancient times, communications in Congo were primarily oral and long distances, with messengers travelling from town to town on foot and by pirogue. At that time, messengers and public speech were widely used throughout Congo. In addition, authorities used instruments such as the flute, the slit drum, and tam-tam to convey special messages. "Talking drums" were a major form of communication among Congolese societies. The drum, usually a hardened tree trunk or other form of hollowed wood, imitated the tones and vowels of some of the Congolese languages in many ways. As a result, the drums could be understood by ethnic groups speaking different languages.

Modern means of communication were introduced to Congo during the colonial period in the mid 1900s. For a long time the radiotelegraphy was the only modern means available. Then more complex means, such as the radio, was introduced. As a result, most Congolese received information through radio, which was historically the most accessible and most popular of the news

media. Radio broadcasting service has been present in Congo since its intro-
duction by Catholic missionaries in 1937. The colonial government followed
suit in 1940 with the creation of the official Radio Congo Belge (RCB).
Beginning in 1950, telephone line systems were established in some parts of
the Congo, notably Kinshasa, Bas-Congo (Matadi), and Katanga provinces
(Lubumbashi).

But long before, in 1892, the missionaries introduced the written press to
Congo with the creation of "Minsamu mia yenge" in Matadi, Bas-Congo province. The colonial government quickly adopted its use, and some time later,
businesses also adopted the use of publications. The press in Congo remained
under foreign control throughout the colonial period. However, before independence, a handful of Congolese had established a reputation as professional
journalists and several newspapers, some of which were financed by religious
groups, were published in the colony and, for the most part, continued to be
published in the early years after the independence of the Republic of Congo.

But Belgium's gradual colonial policy, with its restrictive education system,
limited the possibilities of political participation of the Congolese. Their rela-
tive isolation from the outside world led to a slow growth of nationalism.
Nevertheless, Congolese leaders gradually succeeded to disseminate their
organizational policies to the masses through various newspapers. The most
famous of these was "Conscience Africaine," which was one of the first newspapers to employ Congolese in its editorial staff and the first to express Congolese
views and complaints about colonial regime. The newspaper's endorsement of
a monograph by Belgian professor Van Bilsen, according to which the independence of Congo was not for tomorrow but in thirty years' time, prompted
Lumumba and other Congolese leaders to publish a manifesto expressing the
views of the "évolués" for a comprehensive programme of political change. But
the importance of the manifesto was primarily the fact of its publication. The
main reaction came from the group Kasavubu ABAKO. Three weeks later,
they issued a counter-manifesto supporting the "Conscience Africaine" statement, but going further by demanding immediate political rights of association, speech, and press. In addition, through novels, poetry, and other forms
of narrative, Congolese writers have addressed themes such as colonial oppression, ethnic conflict, political betrayal, abuse of power, rebel invasions and
ethnic cleansing.

Patrice Lumumba's success in seducing the people grew by leaps and bounds.
Through newspapers and radio, by delivering speeches from town to town,
from village to village, he touched the hearts of the Congolese. As a result,

these towns and villages were kept in a state of great agitation. Lumumba continued his activities in Congo by mobilizing also the youth and the women, and by realizing gradually positive actions in a way unknown in the Congo. As a result, people began to see each other as brothers and sisters, regardless of their ethnic characteristics. The question of Congo's unity continued to preoccupy Lumumba throughout his short political career.

After the independence of Congo, the Belgian leaders clearly showed their dislike for Lumumba, especially because of his famous speech delivered on Independence Day in the presence of their King Baudouin. So they began to misinform their compatriots living in Congo that something unpleasant would happen to them under the Lumumba's leadership. The Belgian journalists were not objective either. Moreover, even if they had some understanding of Lumumba's politics, even if they were under his spell, they could not write about it, because many newspapers, especially those in Belgium, supported Belgium's presence in Congo and the establishment of a government of moderate Congolese leaders. The result was a mass exodus of colonial administrators who had lost all desire to work under the new order. Patrice Lumumba was certainly against the departure of the Belgians. But what could he do against the Belgian propaganda?

The "Force Publique", the colonial army that had crushed the Congolese population throughout the colonial period, revolted against the Belgian officers who were still in charge after independence. But in most Belgian newspapers, it was written that it was Lumumba's fault. They blamed his speeches and the policies of the MNC for everything that happened in Congo. In fact, it was the words of the Belgian general of the "Force Publique", Emile Janssens, that triggered the army rebellion. The press has completely exaggerated what happened at the time. The Belgian journalists went wild and wrote: Lumumba, the dictator, the first negro of the so-called state, the mad Prime Minister, the ambitious manipulator, the politician of the bush, the negro with a goatee beard, the dwarf, half charlatan, half missionary, etc. In doing so, the Belgian leaders knew exactly that this exodus could contribute to the collapse of Lumumba's Congo. They knew that, during the whole colonial period, they were undoubtedly reluctant to prepare the natives for their future responsibilities in an independent Congo. As a result, after independence, the Congolese were not sufficiently prepared to be in charge of the administration.

In his Independence Day speech, Lumumba said: "Of this struggle, made of tears, fire and blood, we are proud to the very depths of our being, because it was a noble and just struggle, absolutely necessary to put an end to the humiliating slavery that had been imposed on us by force. Such was our fate during eighty years of colonial domination; our wounds are still too fresh and too painful for us to erase them from our memories." It is this speech that has aroused in the Belgians a deeply hatred towards him. The king of the Belgians, Baudouin, was deeply offended when he heard this speech and wanted to leave immediately and return to Belgium. But for reasons of state, he stayed and went to the official dinner where Lumumba gave a speech that was more suited for Belgium. But the damage was already done. By the way, If one reads carefully the whole content of Lumumba's speech, one will understand that he did not threaten to make the life of the Belgians in the Congo difficult. He was only telling the truth about the psychological and physical suffering of the Congolese during the colonial period, especially after hearing the speech of King Baudouin who praised the greatness of King Leopold II, founder of the Free State of Congo, knowing very well that the latter had committed genocide in Congo by killing millions of innocent Congolese, and also the response of President Kasavubu thanking the Belgians for their civilizing mission in Congo. As leader of the majority in the country, he found himself obliged to respond to the king of the Belgians who, by his speech, further offended the Congolese people on the day of their independence. And he made it clear that as the new Prime Minister, he would first be at the service of the Congolese people, but that he was eager to have a good working relationship with Belgium. As we can see, this was simply Belgian propaganda directed against Lumumba in order to weaken him.

But having failed to bring down Lumumba through the mutiny, the Belgian leaders used the Katanga and South Kasai secessions as obstacles through which he could be trapped. Because of considerable United States and Belgium support for the Katanga secession, and the reluctance of the United Nations to use force to end it, Lumumba requested and received military assistance from the Soviet Union in August 1960. By September 1, 1960, ANC troops had successfully invaded South Kasai and were advancing towards Katanga. Frightened by reports of the audacity of these troops, secessionist leader Moise Tshombe appealed to President Kasavubu, his moderate and federalist ally, to stop Lumumba's anti-secessionist campaign. The ANC's military action in South Kasai resulted in massacres of innocent civilians. This critical factor gave Kasavubu the impetus he needed to make the move against Lumumba. UN Secretary General Hammarskjöld cynically exploited these unfortunate massacres as "genocide" against the Luba of Kasai; Kasavubu found it convenient to blame the Prime Minister, while sparing ANC chief of staff Mobutu and the field commanders. Patrice Lumumba, on the other hand, was accused of the sin of communism, and the crime of genocide. For his enemies in Washington and Brussels, this was, at least officially and for propaganda purposes, the last straw. It provided them with an easy justification to remove from power and eventually assassinate a nationalist and revolutionary leader who threatened their neo-colonial interests in the Congo.

Meanwhile, the United States government led by President D. Eisenhower feared that the Republic of Congo under Lumumba's leadership would fall into the Soviet sphere of influence. And for the American government, Lumumba was a person who had been portrayed as a Castro or worse. Therefore, American leaders decided to use their power to end his leadership by all means. When the US president met with his National Security Council on August 18, 1960, after being briefed by his aides on the situation in the Republic of Congo, he asked them if they could get rid of this "guy". For Allen Dulles, the CIA boss, this was a presidential directive to assassinate Lumumba. He then gave instructions to Sidney Gottlieb, the CIA's top scientist, to land in Kinshasa equipped with a deadly cobra venom substance to apply to Lumumba's food or toothpaste. Lawrence Devlin, the CIA station chief in Kinshasa and the man who had recruited Mobutu for CIA, was against this kind of ridiculous adventure, for the best course of action was to work with Lumumba's Congolese rivals to eliminate him politically and, perhaps later, physically.

Yet, with the clarity of wisdom, Lumumba was probably nothing more than a populist and nationalist politician with radical tendencies. He often told European journalists who asked him if he was a communist that he should always laugh if someone asked him that question. Lumumba was very clear: he was not a communist and would never become one. It is doubtful that Soviet ideology or Marxism influenced him. On the contrary, ignoring the Soviets, Lumumba appealed directly to the West for help in ending the secession of Katanga and withdrawing Belgian troops from his country. In fact, Lumumba's travels in search of help took him to the United States, but never to the Soviet Union or Eastern countries. In July 1960, Lumumba went to Washington. Despite not being able to meet with President Eisenhower, he asked Secretary of State Christian Herter for US assistance. Although he was rebuffed at official level, he continued to seek American help in private sector. He signed an agreement with the Phelps-Stokes Fund to recruit African Americans to serve in the Republic of Congo. Lumumba never used his radio to denounce the United States. In August 1960, he told his people to put their trust in the United States as a great friend. He also said that he would send three hundred Congolese students to the United States for training.

But all these initiatives could not change the prevailing perception in the White House that Lumumba was a tool of Soviet interests. The United States wanted external interventions to restore the legitimacy of the central government of the Republic of Congo, but without Lumumba in charge. Therefore, they planned to prevent the political consolidation of Lumumba, arguably the most popular Congolese politician. Moreover, there was no longer much doubt that the United States was the main force behind Lumumba's ouster and assassination. In its attempts to remove him from power, the United States made sure that he could not count on the support of the army, and in this attempt, Mobutu was of paramount importance. In the case of Soviet aid to Lumumba, the UN's actions were also part of a larger propaganda campaign to convince the world public that Lumumba was determined to allow Soviet expansion into the heart of Africa. The campaign was part of the psychological preparation necessary for a major coup in the Republic of Congo, one inspired and supported by the Western powers. For this coup to succeed, the support of the UN Secretary General Hammarskjöld was essential.

The reasons why Lumumba aroused such intense emotion are not immediately obvious. At the time, the agenda for nationalists and politicians was independence and economic freedom, and Lumumba really believed in them. People understood that these were not just empty campaign slogans designed to win votes, but that here was a man who was not willing to compromise on his country's independence and on his principles. That is why they were all against him. It was not just the press. There were also the religious missions, especially the Catholics, who were strongly opposed to Patrice Lumumba. And even other politicians, who defended the same policies, were not attacked in the same way. It was only the propaganda of the Western powers and Belgium. Lumumba's point of view was not exceptional. He was for a unitary Congo and against division of the country along tribal or regional lines. Like many other African leaders, he supported pan-Africanism and the liberation of colonial territories. He proclaimed his regime to be one of "positive neutralism", which he defined as a return to African values and the rejection of all imported ideology, including that of the Soviet Union.

The role of music in the politics of Congo

In Congo, music and dance are powerful means of expressing reverence and praise for people of power, such as a political leader, a tribal chief, a president, a king, a religious leader, etc. They are also a primary means of entertainment at various social gatherings.

Indeed, in the traditional Congo, musical styles varied according to political and social styles. Where there were strong kingdoms or great chieftaincies, praise music for the king or the paramount chief was more complex and elaborate. This was the case among the Mangbetu who live between the Uele and Bomokandi rivers in Haut-Congo. Court music reflected the power and the splendour of the king. In particular, King Mbunza, who reigned in the 19th century, was a great king. Huge musical instruments were found in the king's court. Instruments symbolizing his power could not be found anywhere else, such as the double iron bell, large ivory horns, and certain types of slit drums. Numerous and imposing musical groups performed for the king, included some famous musicians personally invited by the king to live at court while earning a living from the land provided by the sovereign. They played certain musical instruments for various purposes. The double bell announced the king's departure for a battle, his visit to a subchief, or his return to court. Some types of slit drums, which were played individually or in combination, served many purposes such as praising the king's power, reinforcing the authority of the subchiefs as representatives of the king. Slit drums transmitted messages about major life events such as birth, death, a great feast, a major hunting expedition or a war. During dancing parties, slit drums could be used to request drinks for the musicians or to invite a spectator to dance. Whistles were widely used by court musicians and commoners for a variety of purposes.

Indeed, during those days, Congolese made and listened to music that was intimately connected to the visual and dramatic arts as well as the broader fabric of daily life. Drums and dances were part of all festive occasions, whether greeting or promoting a political leader, campaign rallies, political demonstrations, fooling around in the village or performing at a cultural event. Because of the importance placed on rhythm, drums were perhaps the most important of the traditional instruments and some had long been used to communicate and make music. These talking drums could be heard over long distances and conveyed their messages using a range of tones and keys that mimicked those of spoken words. In some traditions, the slow, rhythmic drumming meant death. A slow rhythm played five times signified the death of a chief; four times, the death of the chief's wife; and three times, the death of the chief's son. A fast rhythm meant urgency and the need to return home immediately. Two types of specialists were involved in the transmission of messages by the drum: those who sent them from the origin and those who decoded and interpreted them at the destination. Sometimes, relay stations transmitted the messages by the drum to following villages.

Moreover, each Congolese tribe has its own way of playing music. And these traditional tribal musics have diverse instrumentation, varied rhythms, colourful melodies, inspiration and assembly of words. The main instruments used in traditional Congo are drums, whistles, flutes, horns, metal bells and so on. But, the different tribes of Congo have made a large number of musical instruments that are different from each other and are grouped into four families: membranophones (percussion instruments), aerophones (wind instruments), cordophones (string instruments) and idiophones (instruments that produce sounds by themselves). In colonial times, these tribes used their music to inform their people politically and to make contact with neighbouring tribes. They could also express their feelings about colonial rule on a personal level, for example, by expressing their hostility in folk songs that mocked the colonizer. In my parents' province of Bas-Congo, during colonial rule, songs of discontent with colonial authority contained coded messages inviting people to secret places where they would expose and discuss the causes of discontent and strategies for dealing with it. But the colonial government's response was to eradicate these tribal customs, such as dance, music, languages, and initiation ceremonies. Therefore, the Catholic and Protestant missions forcibly converted the Congolese population to Christianity in its particular European form. The acceptance of Christianity often divided Congolese communities. But despite this, traditional Congolese music has survived. With the first associations based on ethnic characteristics, music played an important role in making the tribal political leaders known throughout Congo. In addition, it has been one of the factors that have contributed to increasing the political awareness of the Congolese.

Even before independence, Congolese artists, especially musicians, showed great interest in politics and social life. More often than not, they acted as social critics. The once popular song "Sooner or later, the world will change (Ata ndele)" was composed by Congolese musician Adou Eyenga in 1955, the year the young Belgian King Baudouin visited Congo for the first time. That same year, statutes were enacted recognizing the emerging Congolese elites known as "évolués" as a distinct social category. Many other signs of the winds of change blowing across Africa were discernible in the Belgian Congo. As the singer says, "sooner or later, the white man will be overthrown, sooner or later, the world will be purified, sooner or later, the world will be turned upside down". In the 1960s, the musicians attacked the behaviour of the new Congolese politicians. In particular, politicians who, overnight, had a lot of money and wanted everyone to notice it. They quickly lost the respect of the Congolese masses whom they wanted to impress, because everyone knew that it was money stolen from the people. Congolese musicians have always played this role of social critics, but sometimes they behave like troubadours in the service of politicians, especially the President. The songs praising this or that political figure are too numerous to mention here.

Congolese modern dance music, referred to as "rumba" or "soukous" in the world, has been popular throughout sub-Saharan Africa since the 1950s. At that time, the music scene in Kinshasa was undergoing great changes. This Congolese rumba has become an exciting rhythmically complex Congolese version of Cuban rumba, a combination of jazz, traditional music and Latin-influenced rhythms. Moving away from simply constructing melodies from the traditional repertoire, Congolese musicians have composed more original works, reflecting the problems of their own lives in song, and some have devoted their songs entirely to the themes of national independence. This evolution can be explained in part by the integration of modern instrumentation from sources outside Africa. This instrumentation consisted of electric guitars, keyboards, trumpets, saxophones, conga drums, piano and western-style drum sets. In addition to radio transmissions, recording companies brought distant musical themes into studios, bars, and individual homes.

This modern Congolese music was already very popular in the 1930s and 1940s in the country, especially in Kinshasa, and was primarily dance music favoured in the large, traditional open-air dance clubs where the orchestra played and the beer often flowed until dawn. The first Congolese musicians to gain popularity throughout the country were Antoine Wendo, Paul Kamba, Antoine Kasongo, Tekele Monkango, etc. Kinshasa was one of the first recording centers in Africa. The first recordings of Congolese music were made from 1947 onwards by the colonial museums. During the 1950s, rumba acquired a typically Congolese rhythmic flavour thanks to the pioneers of modern music such as the composer and bandleader Joseph Kabasele "le Grand Kalle", guitarist "Franco" Luambo Makiadi, the doctor Nico Kasanda, Tabu Ley Rochereau, etc. Consequently, since the 1950s, Congolese music has made all of Africa dance thanks to the spread of Lingala (one of the four national languages of the Democratic Republic of Congo), the power of Congolese radio transmitters that cover a large part of the continent and the undeniable quality of this festive music. The model established by these pioneers of Congolese music has been followed by a number of today's musicians such as Papa Wemba, Koffi Olomide, Evoloko Atshuamo, Fally Ipupa, Kester Emeneya, Lokua Kanza, Ferre Gola, etc, who, thanks to them, Congolese music is more popular than ever in Africa and in the world. They have certainly acquired the ability to arrange and combine sounds that can be produced by the human voice and by musical instruments.

Beautiful songs were written by Joseph Kabasele Kalle who often praised Patrice Lumumba. He defended the cause of national unity and pan-Africanism in most of his famous songs. It is through one of them, independence cha cha "Kimpwanza" which is broadcast in Congo by Radio Congo Belge that the Congolese learn about the independence of their country. This song immediately became the anthem of the anti-colonial movements in all of Sub-Saharan Africa and became the first pan-African hit. By composing this spontaneous and natural music, which is well known throughout the Africa continent and abroad, Joseph Kabasele was referring to the Brussels Round Table conference that opened January 20, 1960. During this conference, the forty-four Congolese delegates led by Lumumba demanded two commitments from the Belgian government before any discussion of the agenda: firstly, that the date of the independence be set, and secondly, that the government consider the resolutions of the conference as binding. The Belgian government conceded on both points and independence was set for June 30, 1960.

Patrice Lumumba experienced the true power of music in politics. Although his political party was not based on ethnic characteristics, he was one of the few political leaders whose name was often mentioned in many tribal songs. In every town, every village he visited, local musicians wrote songs about him, using the most powerful words from his speeches. In some places, he travelled in a "kipoyi", a special chair carried by two people in front and two in the back, a privilege reserved for a very important person. The porters often sing while performing this task. They use three strategies to lighten the burden on their shoulders. The first one is the walk, which is performed rhythmically. The second is a back and forth movement. The porters stop and move back and forth several times before resuming their regular walk. The third strategy is to add a song to both the walk and back and forth movement.

Ultimately, Congolese musicians contributed greatly to Patrice Lumumba's charisma, using the power of music to spread his party's philosophy and ideology throughout the Congo, on the African continent, and abroad. They succeeded in large part because Lumumba became very popular in the world and it was he who won the elections and became prime minister at independence. After his assassination, many world-renowned musicians, including Americans and reggae musicians, wrote songs about him. They praised Patrice Emery Lumumba for being a great asset to the Democratic Republic of Congo and Africa, a very charismatic leader who died too soon.

CONCLUSION

ON JUNE 30, 1960, THE Belgian Congo became an independent state under the name of Republic of Congo. The Belgians were willing to leave Congo in a relationship of political and economic dependence on Belgium that could last a hundred years. Indeed, the Belgians were quite willing to cede political power to the Congolese political leaders as long as they remained in control of the vast economic resources of the provinces of Katanga, Kasai and Kivu. Therefore, throughout the colonial period, they did not really care about preparing a Congolese elite capable of taking over the administration. On the contrary, on June 30, 1960, it was as if they had put a Congolese leadership at the wheel of a car driving at 200 km/h, knowing that it had never driven. A real apprenticeship!

However, what has hurt Congolese political leaders the most is their lack of training in economics and finance. During the colonial period, the Belgians were unwilling to establish universities with strong economics and finance programs, or to offer scholarships for study abroad in these disciplines. Instead, they created a legal class of "évolués" who would be better educated, better trained in skills, better housed and fed, and more modernized in terms of acceptance of Christianity and other attributes of Western civilization than their compatriots. Nevertheless, the "évolués" were in fact political eunuchs. They were to be prevented from developing political aspirations. Parties and other associations that might become political were banned until virtually the eve of independence. School education stopped abruptly at the end of secondary school for everyone except priests.

Indeed, it is estimated that there were only a dozen university graduates in a society of 16 million people in 1960, the year of independence. Although Congolese were trained to operate most of the complicated mining machinery, there was not a single Congolese in a supervisory position in any of the country's mining operations. The end product of this enterprise was a Congolese who was not Belgian, who was no longer tribal and who was only partially modern. The "évolués" had become virtually strangers in their own society. Despite the promise that education and a transformed lifestyle would bring them improved status and greater material rewards, they have in fact become almost "non-persons", caught between two worlds. Indeed, the "évolué" was expected to remain in psychological and political limbo with no future. Congo was destined neither for independence nor for incorporation into the Belgian state; rather it was to have an association with Belgium in a subordinate status, for a hundred years. Despite its plans, the Belgian experiment could not be isolated from the forces that were manifesting themselves in other parts of the African continent and leading Africans to demand political independence. Belgium's delay in creating relevant territorial institutions for the Congolese, its reluctance to allow them to identify with the developing national community, and its ban on political parties until about two years before independence explain in large part not only for the explosive nature of the birth of Congo as an independent state, but also the many problems that plagued Congolese society.

Originally representing their tribes, Congolese political leaders have become deputies elected primarily by people from their own tribe. These new politicians naively thought that by wearing glasses and carrying pens, they would look intellectual. In reality, their primary goals were not to improve the standard of living of the Congolese people, nor even that of their tribesmen. They only cared about making a good living and making a name for themselves as politicians in the newly independent Congo. It was this class of politicians who, after independence, led the country into a civil war that left millions dead.

Patrice Emery Lumumba constantly spoke of independence and national unity to these tribal politicians who were only interested in power to exercise it over their brothers and sisters. He tried to talk about the revolution to millions of men and women. Arrived too early on the political scene of his country, he was like an alien speaking a language that nobody could understand. Lumumba died because he was ahead of his time. He was surely the given genius who arrived too early. He was a great leader who did not have the opportunity to exercise his leadership skills. During his time as Prime Minister, he did not have the chance to lead the Democratic Republic of Congo because the Belgians and especially the Americans decided otherwise. He was assassinated because he wanted to change things, first of all the monopoly of wealth.

Anyway, Patrice Emery Lumumba has become a hero and martyr to many people around the world since his assassination, and many Africans still believe in his dream of an Africa united in the pursuit of its own political interests and economic development. His name has been exceptionally given to streets, schools, and universities in many countries around the world, for example the Patrice Lumumba University in Moscow and films have even been made about him, for example, Raoul Peck's film about Patrice Lumumba, "Death of a Prophet", has been shown in cinemas around the world.

Patrice Lumumba is certainly one of the legendary figures of modern African history. Like Malcolm X, he is remembered less for his lasting achievements than as an enduring symbol of the struggle for self-determination. He is described as a giant, a devil, a mystic of freedom, the Abraham Lincoln of African politics, and a prophet. A prophet who foretold the future, but the future died with the prophet. In Congo, in Africa, it is said that a giant, a baobab fell that night in the province of Katanga, and the water that falls from the heavens, the water that falls from the eyes, the water that flows into the river, all these waters cried out plaintively where death had the face of a prophet. Indeed, Patrice Lumumba is called a prophet by many people around the world for various reasons. But, I think he is a prophet especially because of his death which mysteriously reminds that of Jesus-Christ. As Jesus-Christ was betrayed by one of his close friends Judas, in the same way, Lumumba was betrayed by Mobutu, one of his close friends; Jesus-Christ was killed with two other people by his side, in the same way, Lumumba was killed with two other people by his side; Jesus-Christ died at age of 33, almost like Lumumba died at the age of 35. Both were publicly humiliated and died painful deaths, and their bodies were never found. What a coincidence!

Whatever is said now, today his sons and daughters around the world weep, without ever having known him. His message has vanished, but his name remains. Should the prophet be brought back to life again? Should he be given the floor one last time? The prophecy of Patrice Lumumba will not be silenced until the Democratic Republic of Congo and all African countries have achieved their second independence where the promises of the first one must be fulfilled.

"History will one day have its say, but it will not be the history that is taught in Brussels, Paris, Washington or at the United Nations, but the history which will be taught in the countries freed from imperialism and its puppets. Africa will write its own history, and to the north and south of Sahara, it will be a glorious and dignified history."

Patrice Emery Lumumba

References

Histoire du Congo, Robert Cornevin.
Rise and Fall of Patrice Lumumba, Thomas Nkanza.
Lumumba's Congo, Washington Okumu.
L'Afrique noire est mal partie, Dumont R. Paris, Le Seuil.
Zaire what destiny, Kamkwenda Mbaya.
The Rise and Decline of the Zaïrian state, Crawford Young, Thomas Turner.
The Crisis in Zaïre, Myths and Realities, Georges Nzongola Ntalaja

www.ingramcontent.com/pod-product-compliance
Lightning Source LLC
Chambersburg PA
CBHW070109070426
42448CB00038B/2350